*Punting in Oxford*       *1*

*Techniques of Punting*       *54*

*The History of Punts*       *102*

*The history and techniques of*

# PUNTING

R·T·RIVINGTON

*in Oxford*

25/04/20.

OLEANDER PRESS

To Lav.

In preparation for the ride down the River Charvell, please become familiar with the history and techniques of punting.

Have fun hahaï

Lots of love
Dada xxx

The Oleander Press
16 Orchard Street
Cambridge
CB1 1JT

www.oleanderpress.com

A CIP catalogue record for the book is
available from the British Library.

ISBN: 9781909349629

Designed and typeset by Hamish Symington
www.hamishsymington.com

Printed in England

# Punting in Oxford

## *Until 1900*

OXFORD IS SITUATED high in the Thames Valley, north of the line of hills the river passes through, between the Berkshire Downs and the Chilterns. Oxford was to some degree cut off from the main activity of the Thames. At one time in the middle ages it was believed that Henley might surpass it in importance as a town because the river above Henley was then unnavigable. In spite of river improvements and the building in the 17th century not far below Oxford of the first pound locks on the Thames, Oxford remained somewhat isolated as a river city except from about 1790–1860 when the Oxford canal had opened and was adding to the activity of the river. Oxford still seems to remain in a different part of the country from the rest of the Thames.

The interest in punting on a river is usually very local. Men at Oxford today, though understanding it is the practice or even a tacit rule to punt from the Oxford end of the punt, may not expect to know why. They would be unlikely either to know anything of punt racing, or even of the existence of best and best punts. They would not expect to know that most of the punts at Cambridge are now short and double-ended. Sport on the river at Oxford usually means rowing. The great rowing event of the year is Eights Week in the second half of the summer or Trinity term when up to 120 college crews row bumping races, each chasing the boat ahead, in several divisions, for four consecutive afternoons (called "nights"), competing for the place at "the head of the river", or for the best place in the order below it. When Eights are over, the keener or better oarsmen prepare to take part in Henley Royal Regatta, held three or four weeks after term ends, and then the main rowing season is over.

Punting at Oxford is treated as a leisurely activity or idle recreation, even by the best watermen, appropriately, for the river punted on, the Cherwell (pronounced "Charwell"), is not suitable for more than this. The Thames, the better river for punting on, as the Isis and even more as the Upper River, is used and sometimes over-used for rowing and the latter also for sailing; moreover all the Thames suffers from the wash of motor boats. On the whole, oarsmen do not give consideration to punting as a form of watermanship; skill in watermanship is of comparatively less importance to modern oarsmen than other requirements and does not appeal to all of them.

The name Isis was used for the River Thames in the vicinity of Oxford certainly as far south as Dorchester and perhaps for that part of the river above the "Upper Thames" which began downstream at the London Stone at Staines; users of that term would rarely expect to refer to anywhere above Henley and beyond the gap through the hills. The river below the gap is sometimes now called the Middle Thames. William Camden wrote of the name of the river, "perhaps it may be safely affirmed that it never occurs in any charter or authentic history under the name of Isis which is indeed not so much heard of but among scholars: the common people from its head to Oxford calling it by no other name than that of Thames." Isis fits far more easily into Latin verses, however, than Thamesis. It may be a latinization of Ouse, a Celtic word for water. The use of the name Isis has become confined to the part of the Thames rowed on by college boat clubs, the river from Folly Bridge to Iffley Lock; to use the term now usually suggests that you are thinking of the oarsman's province. The Thames along Port Meadow, above the old Medley flash lock, long disused, was called the Upper River, in contradistinction to the Isis.

The first edition of *The Oxford Dictionary of Quotations* (1941) includes only one quotation about a punt, from Matthew Arnold's poem "The Scholar-Gipsy", much used subsequently in undergraduate articles on punts:

> *"Crossing the stripling Thames at Bab-lock-hithe,*
> *Trailing in the cool stream thy fingers wet,*
> *As the slow punt swings round."*

Bablock Hithe, about six miles upstream from Oxford, but nearer by the road through Cumnor, had a large rope-operated ferry. The quotation above is from Arnold's second, revised edition. The third line from the first edition of 1853 read:

> *"As the punt's rope chops round."*

Arnold had lived for most of his first fourteen years at Laleham-on-Thames and the picture in the revision seems to be that, not of a rope ferry, but of the more romantic and picturesque sight of a ferry shoved with a pole, perhaps of the Laleham or another ferry. It was said also of Bablock Hithe that in the 18th century Viscount Ashbrook, an undergraduate at Christ Church, married the ferry girl there. (A "hithe" is a place on the river for landing goods.)

The third edition of the *Oxford Dictionary of Quotations* (1979) adds two more quotations about punts; the first is from Dorothy Sayers, also about Oxford, and included in the summary from *Gaudy Night* in Chapter 4, "I admit it is more fun to punt than to be punted, and that a desire to have all the fun is nine-tenths of the law of chivalry", Lord Peter Wimsey not appearing to arrive at the point reached by those Victorians who found the pleasure vice versa, if one assumes Harriet did not look ghastly; the second quotation is from *Finnegan's Wake* and is clearly the older usage of the word for any small boat.

The Thames flows past West Oxford from north to south, from Medley to Osney Lock, before turning east to Folly Bridge, to become the Isis. 18th century prints show many watermen's punts tied up above Folly Bridge. These would have been used up and down the river in preference to road transport, taking goods to villages and hamlets on it, ideal craft on the shallow river. Until as late as 1977, beer was delivered for most of the year by ferry-punt to the Isis Hotel above Iffley Lock, there being no causeway approaching it across the water-meadow level.

Above and below Oxford, the Thames passes along a mile-wide level of meadows or marsh. When the river was high, the level flooded; when low, its streams were fordable in many places until controlled and dredged. Across this level the Thames is formed by three streams. Wytham, Seacourt and Hinksey Stream, all one stream, but named by the villages it passes, is on the far side from Oxford; in 1793, it was suggested it should have been made the main Thames navigation stream as part of the Thames Commissioners' improvements. As part of these improvements, Osney Lock, a pound lock, was built in 1798 and Godstow Lock in 1790. Nearest Oxford is the old navigation stream. The main stream now flows along the side of the present Osney

Island, possibly first cut as a mill stream, improved by the Thames Commissioners. West Oxford lies between these two streams, one of the oldest parts of Oxford, the great Osney Abbey on its far side antedating the university. Because of its position on the river, it was from very early a commercial centre and attracted to it the railway that met the canal here and eventually replaced river transport (though the first railway line had stopped short at and did not cross the river).

A 16th-century causeway, in the 18th century created a turnpike road and now Botley Road, crossed the level. When the river was very high, the whole level would flood; it was not brought under control until this century. William Turner, the 19th-century Oxford artist, has left a painting of the level entirely flooded, with a loaded waterman's punt making its way past Seacourt. A photograph of 1894 shows the road approaching the railway station and going under its bridge completely flooded, with an unoccupied punt (it was the most suitable transport in a flood) beside the bridge.

The establishment of rowing as a recreation for university men in the early 19th century required the means for crews to cross from Christ Church Meadow to the towpath side of the river. To prevent unskilled watermen causing accidents to university boats, the Oxford University Boat Club (the O.U.B.C.) tried in 1843 to prevent unauthorized punt ferrymen from taking up passengers from the Meadow. When Christ Church, as the owner of the Meadow, would not cooperate, the O.U.B.C. Issued badges to punters authorizing them for ferrying and asked university men to employ only these watermen. This plan also failed because the badges were too easily counterfeited. The problem was not solved till 1889, when an overloaded ferry punt caused a fatal accident. The O.U.B.C., by then a stronger body, made a rule that each college boat club must have its own waterman and ferry punt;

over-crowding of the punt was punished with a fine. The O.U.B.C. Also persuaded the Thames Conservancy to prohibit ballast dredging near the towpath, because the holes left made punting difficult. Since the gradual replacement from 1939 of college barges by boathouses, the number of college ferry punts has diminished, because there is less need for crews to cross the river. Several ferry punts still remain in the backwater beside the O.U.B.C. Boat house on the towpath. These are used especially during Torpids and Eights Week, but how much longer they will remain is uncertain. One college wishes to replace its ferry punt used for Eights Week with a motor boat.

From the middle ages, fishermen and watermen in Oxford lived in Fisher Row, houses facing a pre-Conquest mill-cut, the old navigation stream, upstream from the castle and the mill, the latter now demolished. Late in the 17th century two families, the Bossoms and Beesleys settled in its parish, St Thomas's, and by the 18th century both were well established as watermen and fishermen in Fisher Row. A study of the community at Fisher Row including these two families, has been made by Dr Mary Prior in *Fisher Row: Fishermen, Bargemen and Canal Boatmen in Oxford 1500–1900* published by the Oxford University Press in 1982. By the early 19th century, the two families dominated the river and were often engaged in fierce rivalry.

In 1841, the founding of the Oxford Regatta added to the means by which the Bossoms and Beesleys now the two leading families of watermen could compete. In its first year there were no punting events. In 1842 the punt race was won by Samuel Beesley, brother of Abel Beesley whose son, also Abel, was to be the greatest of all punters. In 1843 there were three punting events won by S. Beesley, A. Beesley and J. Beesley respectively. In 1844, S. Beesley again won the senior punting prize. In 1844, like many Thames regattas founded in this period, the

Oxford Regatta was becoming a riverside festival: "On the Berkshire side were numberless stalls, booths and some exhibitions giving the scene the appearance of a fair." In 1844 also, John Tims was a competitor, not successfully, in the watermen's sculling. John Tims was eldest son of William Tims who appears in the 1841 census as a resident of Grandpont (living almost certainly on a barge). His younger brother Tom, born 1839, was to become a celebrated and popular university boat club waterman and founded an equally celebrated business of Tims's at Bardwell Road, so that for forty years in North Oxford after 1901, the name Tims's was almost synonymous with punts. John Tims went to Staines and founded the business still there; his son, also Tom, later built racing punts for the Thames Punting Club. John's grandson Ronald was invited to become a Royal waterman, but had to decline because his pleasure boat business would not allow him its commitments. His great-grandson, Stan Tims, is vice-captain of the Wraysbury Skiff and Punting Club and he rarely misses taking part in regatta punting events.

There was a William Timms who was waterman to the 1st, 2nd and 3rd Dukes of Northumberland at Sion House in Isleworth and a Royal waterman also. He died in 1839 at the age of 92 and left a son William born in 1801, the same year as William Tims of Grandpont. It is possible he is the same William who was at Grandpont (the general area of Folly Bridge). Until the railways were built, the fastest way to travel to London from anywhere as far upstream as Windsor was by boat and there was a regular river passenger service from there. It was the tendency for river families of the Lower Thames to move upstream for work as their requirement or opportunities near London diminished. The increasing demand of the use of the river for recreation was one they could satisfy. However, there was also a family of Tims (or Timms) at Deddington on the Banbury road and William of Grandpont had married a girl from there. Thacker includes Tims in a list of seven "more permanent Riverside families". He includes also Salter, Bossom, Harris (of Laleham) and Purdue. The Harris families of Oxford and of Laleham are not connected. The Tims family believed, without being able to verify it, that some of them had been coach men.

In 1845, the Beesleys again won the punting events at the Oxford Regatta and there was then a gap of twelve years till 1857, during which the regatta was not held; then it continued annually until into the 20th century. In 1860, it took and retained thereafter the title of Oxford Royal Regatta because in that year it was held under the patronage of Prince Edward (later Prince of Wales) then at Oxford.

In 1850, there is however, during the gap in the years the regatta was held, an account of a contest between Beesley and Bossom protagonists reported as a local court case and fought through to the end in a spirit not unrepresentative of some 19th-century sport. Samuel Beesley was often known as "Sampson" (and his son, not a celebrated punter, was christened with that name) *Jackson's Oxford Journal* for Aug. 31, said: "The only case of any interest was one arising out of a punt race on Port Meadow Stream on Friday the 19th July last, when Sampson Beesley and John Bossom jun. of Medley Lock, were matched to punt a certain distance for £2 a side. The stipulation was that fouling would be prohibited and that whichever man was guilty of it would lose the race. On starting, Beesley took the lead, but Bossom came up to him just before Binsey Gate" (Binsey Gate remains a land mark on the towpath near the Perch Inn) "when Beesley finding that Bossom was about showing a good lead and likely to win the race, determined to prevent it and drove him into the bank of Port Meadow, keeping him in that position for about 30 yards. The umpires who were together at that time, decided that in consequence of this fouling the race was at an end and that Bossom was entitled to the stakes. In consequence of bets having been made as to the time of punting the distance, Bossom proceeded onwards to the winning post at Godstow, and Beesley did the same and succeeded by a little management in getting there first, when he and his friends demanded the stakes which the stakeholder refused to give up to him and which he afterwards handed over to Bossom in accordance with the decision of the umpires.

"A bet upon this race was made between Adam Beesley and Luckett and the stakes amounting to ten shillings were placed in the hands of James Stroudley who refused to give them up, in consequence of which he was waylaid by Beesley and his party and compelled to give them up the money. A summons was then obtained against Beesley to answer the charge in the city court; but it was settled out of court and Beesley returned the money and paid the expense of the summons, witnesses, etc, amounting to £2 5s.

"A statement of the case, however, was sent up to *Bell's Life* for their adjudication on it and a decision on that statement was given in favour of Beesley. In consequence of this decision Beesley again applied to Luckett. This led to the action in the Small Debts Court where Beesley sued Stroudley for the money deposited in his hands ..." Beesley lost the case. The report concluded: "Mr Mallam applied to be allowed expenses and his Honour said he should readily accede to this application as he was determined to make those who brought up such trivial cases into court, upon such unsubstantial grounds, pay the costs for so doing ... Thus ended the punting-match affair which for weeks past has been the subject of lively interest to all connected with boating operations ... the decision of the judge appeared to give general satisfaction."

In 1859, when a punting race is next reported at the Oxford Regatta, "the Watermen's Punt Race (was) won by John Bossom, the champion, Sampson Beesley being purposely fouled by other competitors." The Beesleys recovered their ascendancy however. In the year before the first professional punting championship, 1876, the result of the Isis championship for punting at the Oxford Open Regatta was I. A. Beesley jun. 2. J. Beesley jun. F. Bossom was unplaced. John Bossom won the punting race for watermen aged over 40. Abel Beesley was succeeding Samuel (Sampson) Beesley, his uncle, as the local champion. He defeated the first professional punting champion, Ned Andrews, in 1878 and remained uncontested champion until 1886 when an annual professional punting championship was founded at Maidenhead. He won this for five consecutive years, from 1886–90. W.H. Grenfell then persuaded him to resign to encourage other competitors. (Grenfell resigned the amateur championship at the same time, for the same reason.) Beesley nevertheless remained by reputation the greatest of punters. In 1895, he challenged the champion, W. Haines, in the one year the championship was not held, but the challenge was not accepted.

Abel Beesley's house, an attractive 17th century building was pulled down about 1919. Photographs always show fishing punts tied up outside it. The family owned osier beds upstream and Beesley advertized himself as fisherman and university waterman, also. Both Beesleys and Bossoms kept boats and punts for hire above Medley Weir, at the lower end of Port Meadow, more easily accessible from Fisher Row than the Isis, the Beesleys on Port Meadow bank, the Bossoms opposite. Both families were entitled by patrimony to the freedom of Oxford, and may have used and valued the freemen's rights at Port Meadow. Members of another branch of the Beesley family are still watermen to St Edward's School at Oxford, with boats on the Upper River.

For many years Abel Beesley was chief waterman to the Oxford University Humane Society, a society endowed to ensure life-saving facilities of all kinds on the Oxford rivers. A .C. Rough, son of Rough the boat-builder, wrote: "my first memory of Abel was about 1912. At that time the O.U.H.S. Had men stationed at points on the Isis. Abel was stationed at Long Bridges and used my father's boat house as his station. From there I saw him carry out some good rescues of rowers in trouble on the Isis. He was very clever with his punt pole. He could feel the bottom and know what was there. Many times he found bodies when other means had been unsuccessful. On one occasion he brought up a skate my brother had dropped in the river. He made a special pole and iron for me about 6ft long when I was about nine ... Abel's style of punting was as follows. The pole was lifted upright and dropped vertically about a foot in front of the body. On striking the bottom, the pole was thrust behind by both hands, not in little pushes, just one sweep. The pole was lifted in three movements and dropped again. The punt was steered by pushing on the bottom, in or out as required." Rough's boat house was burnt down in 1913 by suffragettes. After rebuilding, it was used by the O.U.B.C., Tims and finally by Hertford College.

In 1928, In *West Oxford*, a history of the parish of St Thomas, by T.W. Squires, included an account of Abel Beesley, "a famous champion Punter of England.... He first challenged for the title in 1877." (The match took place in 1878.) "Great interest was taken in the event not only in Oxford, where 'Abel' – for so was he familiarly known by hosts of friends, rich and poor – did his training, but also in the professional rowing world. He was then practically unknown outside Oxford, but in the race punted in great style and won easily, thus setting the seal to his fame as the foremost professional punting expert. He held the championship until 1890, when he retired still unbeaten. The cause of his retirement was due to the fact, that so long as 'Abel' was in the field very few competitors would oppose him. The entries were gradually dwindling when, at Lord Desborough's suggestion a testimonial was got up for the holder, who then retired, and the next year the entries increased considerably. He also won the open punting championships at Sunbury and Twickenham regattas, and as a punter was in a class by himself and it is doubtful if there will ever be his equal. Many feats have been recorded of his strength and skill as a punter, and on one occasion, at Maidenhead, a match was arranged in which the champion had a billiard cue as a pole and sat instead of standing in the boat. His opponent was equipped with a proper pole and stood in the usual position, but lost the match and the accompanying wager. In 1910 great interest was taken in his match with a steam launch, holding five passengers. On this occasion 'Abel' used a two-foot wide boat, with dry wells, and punted from the Meadow side, the course being on the Upper River between Medley and Godstow, half a mile in length. Quickly establishing a strong lead, he was an apparent winner from the outset. The launch, even with full steam up, never seemed to have a chance. The official verdict for the winner was a length of 110 yards, the time registered being 4 mm 12 sec ... When Mr Beesley died he was holding the position of Chief Officer of the Oxford University Humane Society, in whose service he had been waterman for forty-seven years." Abel Beesley married the daughter of the waterman of the Perch Inn at Binsey at a time when the transport of goods to Binsey was easier by water than by road. His two sons were not successful as watermen. Born in 1851, Abel Beesley died in 1921 and was buried in the churchyard of St Thomas. T.W. Squires also said of Beesley: "Amongst notable punters whom he trained for the Amateur Punting championship was the present Lord Desborough (then Mr W.H.

Grenfell), and it is said that many were the fine tussles these two had in their trials. Lord Desborough became one of the finest punters who ever handled a pole." Before persuading Beesley to resign after his fifth successive win, Grenfell seems to have called for some hard training from Beesley (possibly an added inducement to retirement). *The Lock to Lock Times* reported after this race: "Beesley was glad when the contest was over and the stringent rules of training at an end. How he enjoyed his 'liquor' in the saloon of *The Queen of the Thames*, and how delighted was he to once more feel a cigar between his teeth. 'No more running round the park every morning, Abel!' said Mr Grenfell to the champion. 'No sir,' replied Abel, with a hearty laugh and a significant wink, 'none of that tomorrow morning!' Prior to the championship meeting, Abel had run for a certain number of times round Mr Grenfell's park to 'get into condition' and he was not likely to escape this training while under the eye of such a veteran athlete as W.H. Grenfell."

Punting stern first is traditional at Oxford. It is mentioned by Leslie in 1881 as part of the technique of "pricking" a punt (i.e. punting standing still), as contrasted with running a punt: "There is another style of punting, much used at Oxford for light punts, which is done by standing in the stern, or on the till, and pricking the boat along. This method looks very pretty, and if the passengers are placed in part of the well, a punt thus propelled much resembles a gondola." Leslie adds that it is laborious for a heavy punt but very useful in a confined space "as the steering can be accomplished with greatest nicety." This is true; for if the punt is moved at the right speed, that is to say slowly with respect to its momentum, it can be moved forward, back and sideways without the pole being removed from the bottom. Standing on the till to punt is a practice that would have been discouraged by professional Thames watermen, and may not have continued for that reason.

Grenfell wrote of Beesley punting stern first as if it were something of significance, reporting that Andrews, the first champion, had lost to "Abel Beesley, of Oxford, who stood still and pricked his heavy punt, stern first, downstream" and thereby "the supporters of the old style of running received a rude shock". In pricking a punt, Grenfell credits Beesley with the development of the after-shove, calling it the "long-shove": "The long shove, its highest development, came from Oxford, having been evolved by the Beesley family, Abel of that ilk." For pricking a punt, Grenfell says, "the secret of it is to keep the body upright, not to bend over the pole, and to finish the stroke well out." We do not know precisely why Grenfell should mention Beesley's punting stern first. He might have included it because he regarded it as an Oxford practice; alternatively, it should be easier to prick a fishing punt stern first. But we do not know if Beesley stopped up his punt on turning and punted bow first upstream. Tagg also might have punted stern first in 1877 during the first championship match when he punted from the swims, pricking his punt. Writers on punting gave Beesley credit for establishing pricking as a technique, but this was only for racing. He certainly developed and perfected it as a racing technique; but pricking had always been used for handling a punt when it was appropriate.

Between 1880–1900, the great boat builders of Oxford and some smaller boat hirers kept punts for hire mainly in the vicinity of Folly Bridge on the Isis; Salter, Rough, Talboys, Tims, Harris. These were of the fishing punt design, though gradually being replaced by new saloon punts. In 1895, Henry Taunt gave the width of punts for hire at Folly Bridge as 3ft 6in, showing them to be of fishing punt design. Lady Margaret Hall had a punt of this design in 1896. Saloon punts seem to have been late in coming to Oxford. When pleasure punts first went to Cambridge in the early 1900's, they were of course all of the saloon punt design. Jack Beesley had the boat house on the Isis now used by Harris; his name may still be faintly read on the downstream side of it. His rafts for punts were inside the old mouth of the Cherwell at Christ Church Meadow. There were punts for hire at the rollers below Parson's Pleasure kept by its lessee, and at Milham Ford on land now occupied by St Hilda's College but none at Magdalen Bridge till 1911. A cab-owner (and later a taxi-owner), Hearn, kept punts near Marlborough Road. His son, though never employed as a waterman, was one of the two Oxford winners of the professional championship apart from Abel Beesley. Beesley had tried hard to produce another Oxford winner. His best pupil was H. George, a fine punter who could never beat the Haines brohers during the years of their ascendancy.

Punting from the till, mentioned by Leslie, seemed to have disappeared from Oxford long before punting began at Cambridge. It was not uncommon for men in Oxford who wished to learn to punt to go to college watermen for coaching. This practice may not have been followed at any time in Cambridge, since Thames punts were not the traditional craft the watermen there were accustomed to. Before 1914, it was not uncommon to punt at Oxford very fully clothed, often in a suit and starched cuffs. It was important therefore to keep dry and this could be done by keeping the hands very low and fingers relaxed, a style of punting that has disappeared. From a distance, though the pole moved, the punter could appear almost motionless.

A writer of Eton history observed that two Victorian head masters of Eton, Hornby and Warre, both disliked the "idea of using the river for mere pleasure." Rowing provided a discipline. By contrast, punting at Oxford as elsewhere was associated with pleasure, leisure and idleness. In 1899, A. D. Godley, the foremost writer of Oxford humorous verse of his time portrayed the Isis representing rowing and discipline, in

debate with the Cherwell, representing punting and idleness in verses
titled "A Dialogue on Ethics":

> "Said the Isis to the Cherwell in a tone of indignation,
> 'With a blush of conscious virtue your enormities I see:
> And I wish that a reversal of the laws of gravitation
> Would prevent your vicious current from contaminating me!
> With your hedonists who grovel on a cushion with a novel
> (Which is sure to sap the morals and the intellect to stunt)
> And the spectacle nefarious of your idle gay Lotharios
> Who pursue a mild flirtation in a misdirected punt!'

The Cherwell replies:

> "Just commend me to the patience that can bear the degradations
> Which inflicted are by rowing on the dignity of man . . .
> O it's cultivated leisure that is life's supremest treasure,
> Far from athletes merely brutal and from Philistine afar:
> I've a natural aversion to gratuitous exertion,
> And I'm prone to mild flirtation,' said the unrepentant Cher."

The Cherwell concludes:

> "When the Eights are fairly over, and it's drawing near Commem.
> It is Ver and it is Venus that shall judge the case between us,
> And I think for all your maxims that you won't compete with them!
> Then despite their boasted virtue shall your athletes all desert you
> (Come to me for information if you don't know where they are):
> For it's hina scholazomen that's the proper end of Woman
> And of Man — at least in summer,' said the easy-going Cher."

(Hina scholazomen — in order that we may be idle: since "school" and
"scholarship" are derived from it, the paradox was surely intended.)

The River Cherwell, a tributary of the Thames, has two mouths, the upper in Christ Chruch Meadow and the lower at the Gut. A new mouth was cut in 1883–4, to the point at the lower end of the present line of college boat houses on the Isis. The new cut reduced flooding. The bridge over the upper mouth of the Cherwell was built in 1884. The Cherwell is a narrow, quiet river, more beautiful in its location than the Thames and used only by pleasure boats. The name, pronounced Charwell (with a vowel-change like "Derby"), is often shortened to Char. The Cherwell in Oxford is divided into two levels by a weir just below Parson's Pleasure, a place for men's nude bathing, long established, for there had been an attendant there from at least 1832. Henry Taunt tells us that in 1692, it was called Patten's Pleasure and the name is corrupted from this. The river passes between screens to hide the bathing place. When later rollers were installed beside the weir to move craft easily from one river level to the other, ladies landed above Parson's Pleasure and walked round to rejoin their craft at the rollers, the men taking the boats through the bathing place. Before this there was a wooden water-slide for watermen who had to haul boats from one level to the other. The two levels were called the Upper Cherwell and the Lower Cherwell.

An ornithologist, W.W. Fowler, who was an undergraduate at Oxford in 1870 and lived subsequently at Kingham in Oxfordshire, described the Upper Cherwell about that time, "When ... the Cherwell was an almost unknown river. I well remember my first voyage of exploration beyond Parson's Pleasure. Just above the bathing place we were hailed by a man in a punt, who demanded sixpence for admission to the higher reaches; this my companion, a barrister from London of powerful build and obstinate character, sternly refused to pay, and we went on. But on our return we found the enemy's punt moored across the stream, and himself armed with a long boat-hook to arrest our progress. Then ensued a terrific naval battle, watched with immense delight by bathers drying themselves on the bank, who naturally took our side and cheered loudly every charge we made..." The university used to let the fishing rights of the river to fishermen, and perhaps the fisherman believed either that he also had the navigation rights or that Fowler's party was going to fish. Fowler does not describe the passage at the weir at Parson's Pleasure; presumably his boat used the water slide. Fowler says that later, "the Cherwell began to come into fashion, and to lose the last syllable of its name — for familiarity breeds contempt even in the use of language, and I doubt whether many undergraduates are now aware that it ever possessed a second syllable. Dons began to keep boats on its bank: ladies' colleges claimed it as their own, and all the summer term it became a scene of enjoyment for pleasure-loving youth and pensive middle age."

In 1882, a committee of four including A. L. Smith, once bow oar in a head of the river crew and later Master of Balliol, and Prof. Max Muller (who was married to a Grenfell) asked St John's College for a lease for a boat house site on the Upper Cherwell. Their letter said, "The right of boating on the Cherwell has been expressly stipulated for members of the University in the University's late, and in its recently renewed lease of the fishing rights to other parties; and it has in times past been largely used and much appreciated during the long Vacation by the residents ..." They complained of trespassing and of vandalism to boats, giving this as the main reason why they wanted a secure boat house. The Upper Cherwell Boat House was therefore built as a shareholders' company, holding twelve boats. The St John's College bursar however warned the committee that "the University rights do not extend beyond Great Wisley corner in the parish of St

Giles – that is the corner above the Ferry where the river turns to the East [*sic* – West?]. Members of the University boating on the river beyond this point equally with other would be trespassers ..." The navigation here belonged to Summer Fields and the school was jealous of its property and would sometime stop boats, perhaps because the boys bathed naked. This did not deter undergraduates from making the day's outing by punt to Islip. Islip, seven miles above Oxford, is not as is sometimes said, on the Cherwell, but on a tributary, the River Ray, half a mile above the confluence. In 1888, Lady Margaret Hall had a boat at the Upper Cherwell Boat House; in 1890, Somerville Hall had a boat and St Hugh's Hall a half-share in a boat.

In 1892, another group asked St John's for a lease "on the understanding that the shareholders in the new Boathouse would all be occupiers of houses on the College Estate and all members of the University, this latter qualification being required ... by the Curators of the University Parks – the Boathouse is to be of similar construction to that lately erected and certainly not of large size." This was built alongside the first Upper Cherwell Boat House, on the bank of what is now the Dragon School's playing field. Later Somerville had a boat house just below the Isle of Rhea, at the corner by the Dragon School field, where there was once a women's bathing place; for a time St Hugh's had the old Upper Cherwell Boat House. When the colleges no longer used them, Tims's took them for their punts' winter storage until they fell down. There were probably some other small boat houses in the area also.

All this development of the river by the university for pleasure must have encouraged it to improve the facility for moving boats between the Upper and Lower Cherwell, and it installed the boat-rollers at the weir below Parson's Pleasure. Later, Henry Taunt said the Cherwell could be enjoyed "from its mouth to Islip which thanks to the courtesy and public spirit of the University of Oxford has been made available through the erection of a roller slide for boats ... and the implied permission to all who know how to behave themselves to boat on the private water of which the river throughout its course consists."

In 1896, Lady Margaret Hall, encouraged by a gift for the purpose, built its own boat house on the site of its present one, next to the land-drain used as a backwater dividing the college garden from the University Parks. The Victorians had already recognized punting as a recreation especially suitable for ladies. Their boat house later had two skiffs, two canoes and two punts. Members of the college who used the boats had to pass tests of competence before taking them out alone; when qualified, they took the title, as appropriate, of "skiff captain", "canoe captain" or "punt captain": a punt captain to pick up in three and use a half shove and a back-shove.

Until the installation of the rollers below Parson's Pleasure, probably in the mid-1890's, the Upper and Lower Cherwell were virtually separated. The increasing use of the Upper Cherwell for pleasure boats by North Oxford (Norham Manor Estate) residents mainly associated with the university, led to this important river improvement. In 1901, it was followed by a second major improvement, the establishing of Tims's (the Cherwell) Boat House beyond Bardwell Road. The family's name was often written Timms, but not by the family. Taunt, however, had used the spelling Timms in his guides.

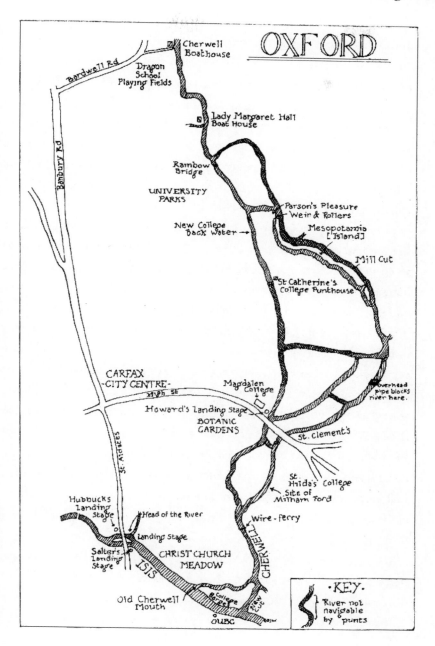

TOM TIMS WAS a celebrated and popular Oxford University Boatman, son of John Tims who had worked for Salters and lived on the Green Barge beside Christ Church Meadow, where university boats were stored before the building in 1881 of the O.U.B.C. Boat house on the other bank farther downstream. In 1901 with encouragement and support from residents of North Oxford in fulfilling a popular demand when punts were reaching their greatest popularity, Tom Tims took a 21-year lease from St John's College for a site for a landing-stage beyond Bardwell Road: the lease was renewed in 1922 and 1943, but relinquished in 1964. Tom Tim's only daugher, Ada, married a young builder's foreman, Harry Walker, and the management of Tims's was placed in the hands of the Walkers. In 1904, the present boathouse was built. Over the centre of the boat house are Tom Tims's initials. The foundation stone has the initials S.L.W., those of Sarah, the Walkers' eldest child, with the date 1904. Tom Tims Walker, the eldest son, always called "Timmy", managed the Cherwell Boat House with Sarah. The second son, Harry, was boat builder at Tims at Long Bridges, formerly Rough's boat house. The youngest son was Arthur John who in the 1930's managed the boat house at Manor Road. The new business was not popular however with its nearest neighbours, the Haldanes upstream at Cherwell, a house once on the site of Wolfson College, or the Dragon School below, then know as Lynam's. The many punts passing their river banks must have seemed an intrusion.

Mrs Haldane, a formidable Scottish lady, mother of J.B.S. Haldane, described the river at the time: "At the end of the century there were no boats on hire above the rollers, and only one private boathouse containing nine boats each of which was shared by two households." (This was until

1892.) "It was not till quite ten years later that the Tims family built its wharf, and started hiring out boats and punts; when this happened, we all felt much aggrieved. Small boys at Lynam's made exciting plans to scuttle or blow up the boats! When I was told about this I said that Mr Tims was a very rich man and would be able to replace each fleet, however often they managed to scuttle it ... The town never appeared during term, and only very occasionally in vacation." Punts then almost entirely replaced skiffs on the Upper Cherwell.

There is a description of the Lower Cherwell at this time in a novel, acknowledging some debt in its concept to *Verdant Green* and published in 1907, *Barbara Goes to Oxford* by Barbara Burke, the pseudonym for Oona Ball. Two young ladies go to Oxford for three weeks in the long vacation to explore it alone, but unexpectedly meet both incipient dons and senior dons all of their acquaintance, who act as their guides. On their second morning, however, still alone, they look for the river: "We set off early this morning for the lower river, that is the part below the town, where we hoped to hire a punt. Long afternoons on the water were to bring us that peace with an Oxford flavour which is what we have come here to seek. A punt seemed to answer all our requirements – for me exercise, for Brownie perfect rest, combined with such absolute safety as should satisfy an anxious aunt. Mrs Codlicott (their landlady) told us that we should arrange to keep it at Parsons' Pleasure and shouted aloud for 'Mr Cox!' (the attendant) as Mrs Codlicott had instructed us to do. We could hear the joyous shrieks of the bathers behind a row of wooden sheds. We made our little plan, and then we went down by the college barges. Here we engaged a punt, a charming light one with ample cushions. The *Pons Asinorum* was ours to have and to hold as long as we chose to keep her. I suppose one does speak of a punt as 'she' in spite of its very unfeminine appearance. "I punted

23

along in my very best manner. On we went past the barges, turned into the Cherwell and skirted Christ Church meadows, lying golden in the sunlight. Then up such a lovely reach; Magdalen walks on our left, on our right a lush green meadow, beyond that some low green hills.

"The stream was very narrow and winding as we came out by the path which is called Mesopotamia; we were in the midst of an argument, the mud was thick and deep, the punt pole long and slender. I remember a moment of horrid uncertainty as to whether the pole belonged to me or I belonged to the pole, – and then, I went – plop – into the water. An opportune waterman rowing down the stream picked me out of the mud and set me on board again. He turned about and came up to Parsons' Pleasure with us and helped drag the punt over the rollers, by means of which one gets from the Lower to the Upper Cherwell. Here we tied up our craft and stowed away the cushions, and I dripped slowly homewards feeling very wet and silly." Edward, Prince of Wales, who had been taught to punt by Haines of old Windsor, was said to have punted very well when at Oxford in 1912, and to have been shown a route to climb in his college, Magdalen, using a punt.

In the latter part of the 19th century, there appear to have been no punting events in the Royal Oxford Regatta and the regatta was defunct by 1914. It was restarted in the 1920's without the title "Royal" and without punting events. Punt racing took place regularly however in the Oxford Watermen's Regatta. The races were always handicapped. Between 1893–1897, entries from well known watermen's families included J. Beesley, W. Beesley, C. Harris, G. Harris and A. Talboys. H. George entered and won in 1901, when he was scratch handicap man with G. Harris; after that till 1910 he was the only scratch man. From 1901–1907, the following entered from well known Oxford watermen's families: F. Bossom, W. Bossom, G. Bossom, W. Beesley,

C. Harris, jun., Horace Harris, Wag Harris and H. Walker; from 1910–1912: F. Bossom, W. Bossom, F. Beesley, E. Harris, F. Harris, H. Harris, J.C. Rough. T.T.Walker and H. Tims.

The regatta continued after the 1914–18 war until the early 1930's. It was held on a course from opposite the Pink Post (stolen in the 1950's, to reappear on the Henley course), just below the new mouth of the Cherwell, to the head-of-the-river finishing post below Folly Bridge. It was unusual in that it was punted upstream only, with no turn (probably greatly simplifying the judging of fouls). The races were held in ordinary pleasure punts. One of the winners of both the single and doubles handicap was Fred Andrews, brother of the present university waterman, Albert Andrews. Some Oxford watermen built and kept their own two-foot regulation racing punts to practise for the T.P.C. Professional championship.

Besides serious rowing at Oxford, there were occasionally less serious college regattas with events for canoes and punts. The punts used were 3ft pleasure punts and might also include one-armed punting, dongola racing and especially punting in canoes. College regattas have not been "mixed" since probably the 1920's, and interest in this kind of watermanship, never so competitively serious as rowing, disappeared: in October 1982, on the day after a St Peter's College Gaudy, two dongola crews formed from men at it, including two former Charon Club presidents, with three other crews, held what were probably the first dongola races in Oxford for almost sixty years. After 1922, a repressive vice-chancellor banned O.U.B.C. rag regattas held between Eights and Commem. in aid of the Radcliffe Infirmary. The principal event was "punt races for college eights", almost certainly dongola races with crews of eight. (He failed to ban coffee shops for, among other things, serving "unmanly food".)

25

Serious punt racing was never established at Oxford University. Some men kept their own racing punts privately but they were very few. In the 1950's and 1960's some even less serious punt racing was established till prohibited by the punt-hiring waterman. The strong commitment in Oxford to rowing hardly left time for punt racing. For the publication of *Punts and Punting* in 1982, two best and best punts were brought to the Isis. There is no record of or reason for best and best punts in Oxford before this, and they may have been the first seen on the Isis. There was only one Oxford University Punting Championship, held in 1905, about the time punting reached the height of its popularity. This championship was organized by B.H.B. Symons-Jeune, author of one of the four books on punting, *The Art of Punting*, published privately by him in 1907. Symons-Jeune came up to New College from Eton in 1903; he left his name on his college's books for a number of years but did not take any public examinations. He was probably a grandson of Dr Jeune, Master of Pembroke and vice-chancellor, a Channel Islander, after whom Jeune Street is named and who married a Margaret Symons. Symons-Jeune did not take part in the university championship, so he had gone down or had declined to enter, perhaps regarding himself as too experienced a punt racer. He had won the double punting championship in 1905 with C.R. Mullings, though the result may have owed much to the latter, for Symons-Jeune was beaten in the single juniors event at the same regatta. Symons-Jeune later lived at Runnymede House and wrote books on gardens.

In *The Art of Punting*, Symons-Jeune describes the conventional racing stroke, including the pick up in three; but suggests an alternative method of recovery as well: "the pole is passed from hand to hand by the right hand pulling it through the fingers of the left as far as is comfortable, when the left hand glides up the pole until close to the right, and so on until the pole is in an erect position; thus the hands never cross as in the previous method, and the pole is recovered in a much more slanting position and seems to swing up almost of itself with the motion of the body." This is a description of the recovery when punting with hands low.

However, he warns that pressure in making the stroke can cause wetness: "So many people think it is a sign of good punting to keep dry and not splash the punt with water, and of course it is very useful for ladies punting for pleasure; but this can only be done by punting carefully and slowly, and it is absolutely impossible when travelling fast. In a race, for instance, every one gets dripping wet, and very often nearly an inch of water has to be baled out afterwards." He includes a chapter on ladies' punting, beginning: "One of the most noticeable features in the development of punting during the last few years is the extraordinary number of lady punters to be seen now everywhere on the river, and nothing looks nicer than to see a lady punting really well ... the average lady is distinctly better, or shall we say a less comic sight than the average man, for most ladies seem to have learnt what most men have not, that bending down and giving a violent dig, instead of a finish, is certainly unbecoming if not actually ineffective." He looks forwards to a championship race for ladies, but this did not come about for twenty years.

He has a brief chapter on the punting championship at Oxford in 1905 and its difficulties: "It seems a pity that the competition should not be of annual occurrence ... if sufficient interest is shown to make it possible. It is rather a difficult matter to arrange, as no one knows better than myself: – Firstly for fear of clashing with Eights, and so losing the support of all rowing men; and, secondly, 'Schools'. As a 'Varsity' man myself, I should suggest that a regatta might be held about a fortnight after Eights, which would give any who were too busy to attend to it before time to practise, and would also act as a pick-me-up to those in for schools a week later." Symons-Jeune's Oxford University Punting Championship of 1905 began with preliminary heats on June 16th and the final heats took place on Saturday, June 17th. There were three entries from men at Merton, two each from New College, Trinity, Oriel and Christ Church and one each from Queen's and St John's. *The Field* reported it: "It is to be hoped that the example of Mr B.H.B. Symons-Jeune's in giving a silver cup for competition in single punts will be followed in future, or it would be better still if a challenge cup could be subscribed for and carry with it the championship of the Isis. Although many men go in for punting at Oxford more or less seriously, last week was the first occasion on which any organized competition had taken place. The result was most satisfactory, and thoroughly justified Mr Jeune's public spirit in arranging the affair. One or two men were unable to compete owing to schools and as several of those entered were comparative novices in the art, it was wisely decided to use the ordinary light pleasure punt instead of the regulation 'two-footers'. The course was on the upper river, over a quarter of a mile stretch lying between Black Jack's Hole and Binsey Gate."

Symons-Jeune's comments on the championship were: "The difficulty at Oxford was to find a proper course to practise on, for it is almost impossible to learn anything like correct style in bad shoving, and the Cherwell and in most places the Isis are solid mud yet there are still many places where the bottom is just as good as is to be found anywhere on the Thames. On the Upper River ... there is an unusually good piece of water, ranging from three to five feet in depth, and it was here that the first 'Varsity competition took place last year ... Both

Abel Beesley and H. George, the two well known professionals, had pupils, and a very fair exhibition of punting was the result, considering the short time given for practice. The two finalists were G. Battock of Trinity (the winner) and A.L. Scott, of Merton, both of whom had lessons from the two professionals above mentioned. The course, owing to an error, was nearly three-quarters of a mile long, instead of the usual half mile and the cup was punted for in ordinary punts... It was at Oxford, about 30 years ago, that Lord Desborough and his trainer Abel Beesley, took up punting, and practically established the sport on the Thames; and it is a curious coincidence that the same Abel Beesley should have trained the first 'Varsity winner at the same place last year."

The course was along the straight reach above Binsey Gate. Black Jack's Hole was a river channel forming an island, now disappeared, off Port Meadow; Black Jack, Thacker tells us, was an imaginary ogre invented to discourage boys from bathing there. To Anthony Wood about 1665, it was "Black John's Pitt". The Upper River is the finest stretch of water near Oxford for punting, shallow, with a firm gravel bottom. The river was dredged on the towpath side and the bank built up and widened, probably at the time of the loss of G.M. Hopkin's "Binsey Poplars": in 1879, Hopkins wrote, "I have been up to Godstow this afternoon. I am sorry to say that the aspens that lined the river are everyone felled." The new and higher bank was replanted with elms. By 1940, they had grown to 60ft high, but thirty years later succumbed to Dutch elm disease. The river below Binsey Gate was dredged and banked on the towpath side in the 1920's and 1930's, to complete the river improvement from Godstow Lock to Medley weir. Godstow and Osney locks were rebuilt, Godstow between 1924–8 and Osney in 1931. The new height of Godstow Lock made the intermediate river level at Medley weir unnecessary, and the flash lock, the last on the Thames, was removed in 1930. Binsey Reach was where in the early 1860's, Charles Dodgson (or Lewis Carroll), rowed Dean Liddell's daughter in a pair-oared gig remembering the healing, or treacle, well at Binsey Church where St Frideswide's unfortunate suitor recovered his eyesight, while he telling the story of Alice in Wonderland. Dodgson took a gig for in the 1860's pleasure punts were of course still very unfamiliar craft.

Symons-Jeune's hopes for an Oxford University punting championship were never fulfilled There was no place left for it by college rowing. The Trinity term at Oxford was over long before the season for skiff and punting regattas and the shortness of term did not allow for a new sport to begin in the remaining two or three weeks after Eights. In 1966, a member of the T.P.C. Committee, with the committee's support, wrote to the secretary of the Oxford University Boat Club asking whether there would be any interest at Oxford in arranging some form of punting match with the T.P.C. No reply was received. However, punt racing has its own place after the conclusion of the rowing calendar's principal events and does not begin till long after the university has gone down. Any undergraduate living in the Lower Thames Valley, competent in a pleasure punt who wished seriously to train for punt racing would be welcomed by a skiff and punting club (particularly if he had also had the opportunity to punt a canoe). Hampton School, which has provided several O.U.B.C. Oarsmen recently, is close to the Dittons S.P.C. And the Thames Valley S.C. And has provided them with members; so also have Tiffin and Emmanuel schools. A university punting championship under T.P.C. Rules would be hardly possible without help from a skiff and punting club. If there were a university club interested in punting as watermanship, affiliation to the T.P.C.

Would be appropriate and would provide a liaison with other clubs.

In 1908, Tom Tims began building the residence, fit for a prosperous Oxford tradesman, behind the Cherwell Boat House, but died before it was completed. Difficulties followed with access to the boat house which had been by a footpath from Charlbury Road. In 1910, therefore, to ensure a right of way, the Walkers took a lease of land for, and built, Nos 2 and 4 Chadlington Road. The lease for No 6 they sold. This ensured access from Bardwell Road for both the new road and the boat house.

The second of the three present-day Oxford punt-hiring firms began at Magdalen Bridge, as Round and Faulkner, in 1911. Until 1911, the hardway down to the river beside Magdalen Bridge was used for watering horses. The bottom of the river there is paved or cobbled, the stones being laid for the horses. There was no exit to the other bank. When horse-trams were given up, the hardway was no longer required for their horses. William Round and Owen (known as "Joe") Faulkner, watermen at New College and Worcester, leased the site from the City Corporation for punt-hiring. At this time college watermen who wished to increase their earnings in an occupation that ceased during the long vacation engaged in letting and building punts. There was business to be had from residents and visitors; some of them managed to combine the two jobs in university term. In the 1920's, watermen letting boats around Folly Bridge sent touts into St Aldate's to look for trade. Faulkner also had punts for hire at Milham Ford until 1938; he relinquished the lease to the Corporation and the site now belongs to St Hilda's College. Owen Faulkner's son, J.A. Faulkner, waterman at Corpus, took over the business at this time. In winter the Faulkners' punts were stored in a boat house at the Kidneys below Freshman's Creek, on the site of the present Sea Scouts' boat house, and the Faulkners lived in a house behind it, Ferry House, Meadow Lane, built for them in 1927. At this time there was a ferry punt, shoved with a pole at the site of Donnington Bridge, maintained by the City Council as a foot passenger's free ferry. It was replaced by a concrete arched foot bridge in 1937; the road bridge was built in 1962. The last ferryman was Thomas Rose. He became landlord of the Isis public house on the towpath above Iffley Lock. Beer barrels and other heavy supplies were delivered to the Isis in a ferry punt until about 1977. For a good deal of the year, the land around the Isis is too wet to be reached by lorries and the beer is now brought down the towpath by trolly. The present landlord is Thomas Rose, Rose's grandson and a boat builder, once apprenticed to George Harris.

The Cherwell Hotel in Water Eaton Road, north of Summertown and on the Cherwell just above Cromwell's Meadow, opened as the Cherwell Tavern in 1896. It was rebuilt in its present form in 1900. Its possibilities as a riverside hotel were never realised. The landlord from 1900, Harry Moreton, was also a boat builder. A new landlord took the lease in 1906, the hotel was renamed the Cherwell Hotel, and Moreton remained a boat builder. In 1912, Ernest Robinson, waterman of Balliol College (and later known as "Gramp"), became landlord and in 1918 took on Moreton's business as well. Robinson gave up the hotel in 1923, but let punts from the boat house until 1939. After this the boat business was continued by the hotel landlords. The boat house burnt down about 1922 and the present one was built to replace it. In 1933, with the building of the Cutteslowe Estate adjacent to it, the Cherwell Hotel was enlarged. In 1940, a new inn sign was painted showing a man in straw hat and white flannels falling in from a punt; with the animosity created by the pulling down and re-erection of the Cutteslowe estate walls in

1939, a palpable class-barrier, the sign was said by local residents to represent the forthcoming downfall of the privileged classes. It was elsewhere remarked that the punter was foolish enough to punt from the Cambridge end. Punt-hiring from the Cherwell Hotel boat house continued until about 1967. The boat house remains with the punts, now too decayed to be of use.

Charles Howard, having followed his father in 1907 as a cab-owner at Cherwell Street, St Clement's, at some time left this occupation and became the attendant at a swimming bath at the end of Cherwell Street, behind St Clement's Church, perhaps when cabs were giving place to taxis. Howard began to let punts on the Cherwell beside the swimming pool, combining the two jobs. By 1928, he was also a boat-builder and had more premises a little further down at George Street, now demolished (though the landing steps have survived). When about 1936, Faulkner and Round separated, Round took a shed and landing-stage on the site of the Florey Building in St Clement's. The site was requisitioned from 1940–45 and when released was taken by Howard's son. The family firm remained there till it moved to Faulkner's landing stage at Magdalen Bridge in 1967 and is now in the hands of his grandson and great-grandson, both Charles Howard. The family have occupied four sites on a half-mile stretch of river, moving about 200 yards downstream to a better site at each move.

In 1935 and for probably 10 years earlier, T.R. Woodward, a cabinet maker, owned a boat-house at 43, Boulter Street, St Clement's, the last house on the left. It was a very small business, with not more than a dozen punts said to be let to Exeter College. In 1952, it was in the hands of another member of the family and it closed in 1960. The house is now the property of the university and its landing stage remains attached to it.

In the 1930's almost no men's colleges owned punts. New College had some in the mill cut at Manor Road, known as New Collage backs. St Hilda's College had twelve punts and members of the college, like those at Lady Margaret Hall, had to qualify in watermanship before being allowed to use them alone; they had to pick up in three and be able to steer during the shove, not at the end of it. Some colleges syndicated punts as they do now and some men bought their own or hired them for a term, keeping them at a hiring stage. Syndicates were smaller, for colleges were smaller. It was common for North Oxford residents also to form syndicates for punt-hiring: two or three families would hire a punt for a season and times for its use would be allocated. Tims's, the Walker family's business, expanded in the 1930's. In 1935, they built a boat house above the new northern bypass bridge over the Cherwell, hoping to get business because of its easy access by road, for there was no dual carriageway at first; they had fifteen punts there, but the business did not prosper. Arthur Walker let punts at Manor Road, having taken over the New College landing-stage, on the site of St Catherine's College's new punt-house, and his punts were always cheaper to hire from there.

---

After 1947, the size of the university increased considerably, becoming more crowded and busier, and changed in some respects from the place it had been before 1940. For college and university societies, punts provided excellent places for parties, some decorous, others less decorous: in 1954, "Punt loads of pleasure-seeking Heretics, forgetting their external fight against orthodoxy ... invaded the Cherwell. Dressed heretically and in some cases piratically in clothes that ranged from rugger kit to army tropical wear, the party moored in the centre of the river by L.M.H. To eat and throw each other in the river."

At six o'clock on May morning, from the reign of Henry VII or earlier, the choristers of Magdalen College have sung a Latin hymn from the top of Magdalen tower, high above Magdalen Bridge and the Cherwell. From 1950, the numbers of those who came to listen increased as did the festival atmosphere of the morning. The High Street and the Plain on either side of the bridge were crowded with thousands of visitors. Teams of Morris Dancers, called "sides", met there, for Morris dancing has roots in Oxfordshire. The most advantageous place for listening was in a punt and punts were hired from five o'clock in the morning. The occasion became fashionable; actresses from London arrived for sausage breakfasts. Because of the large number of punts hired, the hiring time was put back to 1.30 a.m. In 1958, *Cherwell* reported, "Orgiastic, riotous all-night river parties were the outstanding feature of this year's May Day celebrations during which a record number of punts were sunk ... for the first time punts were allowed to leave Magdalen Bridge at 10.00 p.m. instead of 1.30 a.m., so more people than ever spent the whole night on the river." Next year punts left at 7.00 p.m. Disasters were expected. In 1962, "After the singing was over one overladen punt began to sink. The occupants jumped into the next, and caused this to sink. It ended with six punts sinking and fifty people in the water. A piano, eccentrically carried into one of the punts, had to be ferried to safety by its keepers".

In 1964, *Cherwell's* report concluded with an ominous note on violence on the river. "There are fewer boaters and bottles of champagne on the river nowadays, and whereas once the well dressed young gentleman would take his young lady for a punt up the river, now the order of the day is jeans and a sweater. Apart from other considerations, one reason for the change in the attire is that few modern undergraduates can punt efficiently and they compensate for this by being prepared in their dress to fall in... The freshmen have been initiated into the noble art of punting and some have now spent a whole night on the river over May morning because 'that's what you do in Oxford isn't it!' The older and wiser among us have given up all night punting ... there is an element of hooliganism and loutishness in the rest ... five punts from Bardwell Road alone were sunk on May morning and not one of these people had the decency to help return them to the punt station. One of the punts was never recovered at all".

Discipline declined further. 1966 was "the most disastrous May morning in years... The havoc started just after midnight... John Evans (Magd.) said: 'Our dinghy ran into two punts packed with town drunks about 1.30 a.m. They boarded us, armed with broken punt poles and oars. They hit out at everything in sight. I was punched in the mouth and others were beaten over the head and body'. ...other damage reported included one punt stuck at Iffley; fourteen missing and various thefts from punts." The limit was reached the next year. The Cherwell Boat House prudently hired out no punts for May morning. For the other boat stations: "Never again ... was the verdict of Oxford punt-owners. Mr. Derek Howard had over £500 of equipment still missing... Other owners are firm if regretful... Only Christ Church undergraduates who have a special arrangement with Salters are likely to be on the river next year ... unless their determination weakens, the other major suppliers, Howards, Hubbucks and the Cherwell Boat House will not be hiring out next year... 'It was wanton destruction; sheer hooliganism,' said Mr Hubbucks. Town youths hurled burning logs and clods of earth at punts passing Magdalen College. One punt was stolen at knife point."

No punt hirers since then have hired out punts for May morning. Even undergraduate colleges that own punts are careful; Magdalen College owning a large number of punts does not now even put them on the river until after May Morning.

The Charon Club, founded as a university club about 1950, may have originated about 1939 as a St Peter's Hall (now St Peter's College) informal club for the convivial sharing of the ignominy of falling into the river from a punt; and later in the 1950's St Peter's Hall members were well represented among the club's officials. The club was founded because of an open challenge to a punt race posted in Oxford in the Michaelmas Term of 1952 by the Cambridge Damper Club. A reply was made in February 1953 by some Wadham undergraduates; however they had difficulty in finding a team, and did not actually accept the challenge till Friday, May I, for a race to take place at Cambridge on Sunday, May 3. There were teams of five, with relays up and down a 300-yard course on the Backs; a L.M.H. Girl acted as Oxford relay baton. Cambridge won, having lost the toss and recommended Oxford the bank with more mud on it. The Oxford team then formed the Charon Club as a university club, registered with the proctors, on May 6. Four of the seven undergraduate committee members were Wadham men. The club's aims were to promote: I. an annual punt race between Oxford and Cambridge, 2. an annual rally ... where wine may be consumed, and 3. the ancient art of punting. A rule said, "members shall have fallen unwittingly from a punt, boat or canoe into a river." The club's motto was *Ecce excidit puppi in undas* (*Aeneid* VI) "Look, he has fallen off the stern into the waves". All women members elected were called batons; the one chosen to take part in the race was called the chief baton, and from 1957, the Queen Baton. Besides the usual club officers, keepers of the punts, of the pole and of the batons were appointed. The club later took some responsibility, *faute de mieux*, for the interests of punting in the university, but its objects first and foremost were light-hearted and social.

Though the undergraduate newspaper, *Cherwell*, did not report the first race, it took the opportunity of noting it in a special article on punting, saying "It has all been done before. Each succeeding year only extends the vicious camaraderie of 'pukkha sahibs' in the world of punts. On the first warm dry day of the Trinity Term, studiously nonchalant freshmen approach the temple of Timms (*sic*) to enter the presence of the Great God Cher. Loudly they creep upstream with crab-like futility, swearing as they go. Debonair veterans in jeans and sunglasses glide smoothly past the novice wallowing in his clumsy circles. Initiation is severe. But inferiority complexes are easily developed; after an hour or so the ordeal of a puntster's basic training is over. He quickly forgets his earlier follies and concentrates on the finer points of an art which has endless possibilities for the gamesman. The languid air of superiority bestowed on a perspiring overtaker, looking as if you could go a lot faster if you cared to; that *legerdemain* which will transfer the pole from near horizontal to a Damoclean poise by one flick of the wrist; frigid hearty advice to a bewildered learner: all these show a mastery of the basic techniques of Chermanship. . . . Clumsiness is perhaps the commonest sight on the Cher; but even this is sometimes studied. The rollers offer opportunity for the downtrodden: inmates of Keble run amok with their punt poles and Wingfield nurses (who can all swim like fishes) fall into the river suspiciously near the fence of Parsons' Pleasure.

"But now a hint of commercialism is creeping on this hitherto carefree sport – The Competitive Spirit – that last infirmity of the noble English mind – has already produced a Varsity Punt Race and will soon reduce the Cher to another, muddier Isis. An excrescence of prefabricated punt houses will soon creep along the Parks bank. And the crowning horror will be Punt Cuppers."

The excrescence of punthouses did not appear. The annual relay-races continued for twenty years. Courses were later about 100 yards long with teams of eight. Their locations changed – below the Victoria Arms, along Christ Church Meadow Bank, on the Backs at Cambridge. Each side had two punts going backwards and forwards between a pair of marks at either end of the course for eight legs. As a punt reached the end of the course, the baton jumped into the other punt already beginning to travel in the opposite direction. There were usually four stake-punts, two at each end of the course. Reaching the stake-punt, the baton had to step onto it and re-embark on the opposite side. The second year the Cambridge Baton fell in "for the benefit of a Fleet Street photographer." The next year the Oxford Baton was pushed in and in years afterwards, all the competitors went in. In 1956, 1000 spectators were reported. In 1957, at Cambridge, 3000 spectators; Oxford lost, when an Oxford competitor lost his pole to a pole snatcher on a bridge on the Backs. This seems to have been regarded as fair play, perhaps because no competent punter need lose his pole to a pole snatcher. In 1959, the Charon Club president introduced a "horizontal recovery of the pole introduced from America." The purpose was partly for amusement and novelty and partly to foil Cambridge pole-snatchers. Instead of making an after-shove, the punter fell flat on his back and made the recovery from the supine. The batons decided they had no confidence in the technique, revolted and issued a challenge of their own to the Dampers. However, the matter seems to have been settled and at least two of the Oxford team used the technique during the race. In the 1960's the club extended its activities to river Safaris and punt jousting contests. In 1968, the programme of events for the Charon

Club *v.* the Dampers Club had become almost a small regatta and in addition to the main event included: I. Doubles punting – Rainbow Bridge to Bypass Bridge and back to the Victoria Arms, 2. Jousting, 3. Damsels' race, 4. One-handed race (considered the most entertaining), 5. Canoe punting. In 1969, *Vade Mecum* gave the officers of the Charon Club as the Grand Maistre of the Pole, the Keeper of the Scrolls and the Guardian of the Koffers and its aims: "To defend the noble and ancient art of punting and to clear the Cherwell of transistor radios and undesirable characters; to defeat Cambridge in the annual Grand Punting Tournament at the Victoria Arms (Marston). Qualifications: to have entered the Cherwell fully clad from a punt (Oxford End)."

The ambitiousness of the programmes may have been the beginning of the fixture's terminal difficulties. More and more punts were being damaged in both regattas and practices. It was customary at the end of the events, for all the participants to fall in the river and all the punts be sunk in a general battle, even before the end of the race in some early fixtures. The control of big regattas was difficult also. After the event of 1973, boat-hirers prohibited the use of their punts for racing or any other kind of competitive events, including the Charon Club's, and there have been no more matches against the Dampers Club since then. Registration with the proctors ceased at the end of the Michaelmas Term, 1974, and the club has been defunct since then. However a group of undergraduates who met the Dampers Club at the end of the Trinity Term, 1982, reformed the club and held their first dinner at the Randolph Hotel in November. This began with the hail to Charon from *The Frogs* of Aristophanes: "kair ō Charōn, kair ō Charōn, kair ō Charōn." The founder of the club in 1953, Peter Goodford, has recently returned to Oxford. The club hopes he will be their senior member. Goodford married a baton.

In 1957 Talboys died, aged over 90, and his business which included punts for hire above Folly Bridge was sold off. In 1958, George Harris gave up his punt hiring business at Folly Bridge; he sold the business except for the punts to W.T. Hubbucks, let the punts for a year to colleges and then disposed of them. Hubbucks has retained the business; the former Folly Bridge toll-house is used for part of it and the rafts are above the bridge. He was helped by his two sons, Paul and Lee. Salter found the other sides of their business more profitable than punt-hiring and did not replace their punts. About 1969, deciding that punt-hiring was unprofitable, Salter took all their punts off the river and stored them; they remain stored, but are now probably beyond repair. However, about 1971, Salter produced two designs of punt made of glass-fibre, an 18ft pleasure punt and a 14ft work or garden punt. The pleasure punt has a 3ft 3in beam: triangular longitudinal buoyancy tanks structurally replacing chines, and ribs moulded to the sides, provide its strength. The punts are produced easily and cheaply from presses, the pleasure punt at about £500, for sale to boat-hirers, colleges and private customers. Like the Nomad and Camford punts, the 18ft punt feels as much like a canoe to handle as a punt; its unusual width gives it greater comparable stability, but makes it sluggish. It has a high freeboard to protect it from wash.

In 1959, a *Cherwell* reporter said "punting as a sport is declining … many firms have had to sell off their punts… A Salter's boatman said, 'we used to have 100 punts but now we are down to 40. A punt costs six times more than in the thirties and a lot of firms have sold off…' Ted Tims, after 58 years of looking after undergraduate boats, lamented: The undergrads haven't got the spending power nowadays… And the clothes they used to wear! None of the sweaters and jeans you see now, but smart flannels, blazer, boater and buttonhole." Ted Tims may

41

have been lamenting also the decline in his distant cousin's business at Bardwell Road. There was no boat-builder at Tims. Sally Walker was trying to increase business by serving tea out-of-doors beside the boat house. The lease was due for renewal in 1964 and the state of the business did not allow for paying a large increase in rent. The rent paid may not have been more than paid in 1922 and an eight-fold increase was asked. The Walkers could not continue. St John's College bought the Walkers' assets in the business and sought a new tenant.

In 1964, J.A. Faulkner, suffering increasing damage to his boats from young people, offered his business at Magdalen Bridge for sale. The boats at Magdalen Bridge, both punts and canoes, were too accessible from the landing stage. Faulkner's offer was accepted by Capt. De Goris, a Greek merchant sea captain, still serving at sea; he intended it as a business for his retirement, to be managed meanwhile by his son. The difficulties at Magdalen Bridge were not overcome, and in 1967 the business was sold to Howard of St Clement's. Howard kept the best of both fleets, closed the St Clement's landing stage and moved to Magdalen Bridge. The punts were kept well out of reach below Magdalen Bridge when unattended and all were padlocked, largely solving the problem of damage and theft.

The lease and the assets of Tims's at Bardwell Road were bought from St John's College in 1964 by Lieutenant-Commander Perowne, R.N. (Retired). Lt-Commander Perowne may have been a romantic who dreamed of what Oxford should be before he came to live there. At any rate, he brought imaginative changes. *Cherwell* reported the change of ownership of the Cherwell Boat House. *The Oxford Times* did not; its space was occupied with plans to build an arterial road through Christ Church Meadows (rejected) and to build the Marston Ferry Road link-road and bridge (accepted).

*Cherwell* said, "The punt station at Bardwell Road has just been taken over, following the departure of Tims from the Oxford scene, by Lieut-Commander John Perowne. When he arrived a week before May morning, he found that of the 120 punts only 40 were serviceable. Despite this he now looks after punts for 20 colleges and he has a waiting list of six more colleges. For the repair of punts, he employs anyone who was ready, willing, and able to help, women included. In all 80 punts can now be used and only six of these are for general hire. The rest are all on block bookings to colleges. Very few colleges in Oxford own their own punts as most find it inconvenient to store and maintain them. The average charge to hire a punt for the term ... makes the cost to the undergraduate for a three-hour period ridiculously small whether you pay according to the number of outings, or, as at Merton whether the cost is defrayed against the whole college." St John's College hoped to let the boat house and the Walkers' house separately, but Perowne insisted on having both; for there would be more problems "if Bardwell Road closes down as seems very likely if Lt-Cdr Perowne does not get the house by the side of the station." But "... if he succeeds in getting the house attached to the punt station ... he plans to turn the area by the side of the boat house into a club. He is not sure about the exact form this club will take and is open to suggestions...."

43

Next year, Perowne obtained a wine licence for the boathouse. Undergraduates might have preferred beer, but that was not Perowne's style. He installed two *flambeaux* at the waterside, eight-foot high gas-lit torches with naked flames, three or four feet long, illuminating the river. He did not form a club, but introduced entertainment. In *The Oxford Times*, he advertised: "Oxford's latest rendezvous – The Cherwell Boathouse – Riverside terrace and bar-wines and aperitifs –

Buffet lunches, Teas and Suppers – continuing the cabaret series – Billy and Joanne, talented folk duo – at 8.45 and 9.45." The entertainment however did not survive. What evolved was the building of a restaurant, the Cherwell Boathouse Restaurant, operated alongside the business of punt-hiring. The restaurant succeeded by the service it provided in its attractive position overlooking the river, and it had become especially valued by its Oxford clientèle for excellent, modestly priced food and has been recommended in national restaurant guides for this. Being independent of the boat-business, its service continues through winter and summer. In summer, however, a large open-sided marquee is erected above the lower landing-stage for buffet meals, to serve those who come to hire and others. Though there is a full licence today, the Cherwell Boat House still chooses to serve wine, as in Lt-Commander Perowne's day, and there is no beer.

The new ownership was a sign of the changing times. Perowne was a gentleman, not a professional waterman as all previous Oxford punt-hirers had been. Though a seaman, he was not a boat-builder. He set to work to repair the boats himself with the help of his large and young family and from the men he began to employ as part-time watermen. His family also helped with the new catering business. Maintenance of punts had been neglected and nearly fifty of the punts in worst condition were burnt. A few years before Tims's had probably had about 160 punts. One of the new watermen, John Mastroddi, took a special interest in punt-repairing and as a natural craftsman began to develop his skill.

Perowne had worked with a full-time staff of only himself, his wife and two daughters. When in 1968 the daughters wished to move, he decided not to delegate to staff outside the family, but to look for a smaller business and later found a bookshop in Pembrokeshire where he is now. Meanwhile he offered the lease and the business as a going concern for £17,000, but could not find a purchaser. It seemed as if the boathouse would go out of business. The lease of the house by itself would be saleable.

A few senior members of the university hoping to save the boathouse and its business formed a consortium to seek the means to do this. Meanwhile a recent graduate of the university, a scientist living in Henley, Anthony Verdin, offered for it. Hearing of the consortium's offer, he approached them with the hope of joining them; since they viewed him as a suitable purchaser and were having difficulty they withdrew.

Verdin took on the business in November, 1968. For a time, this was his only employment; but he then saw the opportunity to set up his own scientific company manufacturing pollution monitoring instruments and this became his principal occupation, as it is today. This business is constantly taking him across the world, but at the same time he manages the punt-hiring and the restaurant together, two businesses that can be complementary, as inn-keeping and boat-hiring have often been combined.

While working full time at the boat house, Verdin realised it would be necessary to recreate the craft of punt-building if the business was to continue. No punt-hirer could go on for ever rebuilding the fine punts built thirty or forty years before. Reconsideration and consolidation were also needed of the new ideas Perowne had introduced. Verdin was furthermore able to secure the freehold of the property ensuring a future for the business. Verdin began to build punts, therefore, helped by the increasing skill of John Mastroddi and by advice on both craftsmanship and materials from Paul Hubbucks. To obtain the lengths of mahogany suitable for the sides of the punt, it was necessary

45

to buy a whole tree trunk and have it sawn up especially to order. Experiments were made with other hardwoods also; but mahogany, the traditional wood, proved the best. When Verdin started his scientific business, Mastroddi continued to build punts on his own. There were small alterations to make them sturdier. The huffs were banded with metal to strengthen them and metal runners were put on the bottoms. But in design, they remained traditional Thames punts and today John Mastroddi is the only builder in Oxford of traditional punts.

For a time painters were fitted to both bow and stern of Mastroddi's punts so that the punt could be tied up from the till or stern, as well as from the open end or bow, saving both trouble and damage when coming into the landing stage; but probably with too much concern for tradition, they are now fitted with painters at the bow end only. Since at Oxford it is customary to punt stern first, it is necessary to come in stern first to tie up; this is more difficult; going out is easy enough from either end.

In a compilation of reminiscences, *My Oxford*, published in 1977, various contributors remember punts. The range of recollection is a usual one: romanticising about, reading in, working in punts, and first trying to punt. For the editor of the book, Ann Thwaite, punts were a "part of Oxford's shimmering surface — the white wine in punts tied up beneath the willows." Lord Boothby, an Eton oarsman and fine golfer, first went on the river with Compton Mackenzie: "One evening he came to dinner with me, and after dinner we punted, with two or three friends, down the river. I couldn't punt. As we went round in circles, bumping into a moored punt first on one bank and then on the other, he laughed so much he nearly fell into the water." For Jo Grimond: "the Oxford of punts on the Cherwell, blossom, carols from Magdalen Tower and crumpets in Magdalen on a misty autumn evening ... — these are the Oxford of nostalgia. They evoke careless unhurried days." John Mortimer, novelist and playwright, who had read law, remembered working in a punt, though he found "learning law enormously dull ... *Tort in a Nutshell, The Basic Real Property, All You Need to Know about Libel and Slander.* I read them ... as we punted down the river." Alan Coren, now editor of Punch, associated punts with books being read in his time, for "in the various waterways around Oxford the punts coagulated sluggishly into logjams as their polers hove to in order to read aloud to one another. Through the mists of spiralling gnat, snatches of Salinger and Scott Fitzgerald filtered from boat to boat... Almost everyone had bought *Doctor Zhivago*, though it would have been possible to put all those who had actually finished it into one punt with no threat whatever to its buoyancy."

---

Almost everyone at Oxford without a dislike for water usually tries at some time to punt, helped by the college system of block-booking punts. An article in *The Tatler* for June, 1982, reported from Oxford: "Everyone punts. It doesn't matter about political views, educational background or how much money you've got."

Usually all undergraduate colleges (and many all-graduate colleges) make arrangements with one of the three Oxford boat-hirers, the Cherwell Boat House, Bardwell Road; Howard at Magdalen Bridge or Hubbucks at Folly Bridge, for the block-booking of punts for their members' use for the whole of the Trinity (or summer) term. Arrangements are usually made by Junior Common Rooms using J.C.R. Funds. Their members then book them in the same way as tennis or squash courts and pay no further charge. By this arrangement, punt-hirers are insured against losses caused by bad weather during the summer term. Some colleges make arrangements with more than one boat-hirer, and have punts in two locations.

Waterside colleges have their own landing stages and punts: Lady Margaret Hall, Magdalen, St Catherine's and Wolfson. L.M.H. Has had a boat-house and punts of its own since 1895. Wolfson has a magnificent, spacious punt-harbour following the example of St John's College, Cambridge, central to the landscaping of the college. St Catherine's has built a fine punt house on the site of the old Manor Road boat house which it shares with its ground-landlord, Merton. At one time annually, on St Catherine's Day, there was a timed punt race from St Catherine's to the Victoria Arms and back, the competitors having to drink a pint of beer there before returning. Magdalen College is unusual in having its own design of punt, made of glass-fibre. The college now has about 24 of these. The design was provided by the college engineering tutor, Dr Bellhouse. The punts are made in a press in Sussex by the company of a friend of his building racing motor car bodies, Nomad Ltd. The design was made with functional considerations particularly with regard to torque, the twist caused by length of body; it has similarities in design and dimensions to Scudamore's Camford punt from Cambridge. The Nomad punt is light, short and handles easily and more like a canoe than a traditional Thames punt, characteristically long and heavy. Like glass-fibre boats, Nomad punts are cheap and easy to maintain Punt-owning colleges are turning away from traditional Thames punts to other designs, usually of a Cambridge type which do not provide the same pleasure to a waterman to handle as that of a Thames punt.

Because of the college block-bookings, it can sometimes be more difficult to hire punts during term time, particularly at weekends, because there are fewer punts left for hire to the general public. From the end of term onwards, there are plenty of punts for hire. In July and August, they are very popular with the hundreds of young foreigners who come to Oxford for English language study. Punting is also enjoyed by some of those who attend about 200 courses and conferences held in the long vacation in college premises; in September, 1982, 300 members of IBM courses for computer data managers each received a copy of *Punts and Punting*, and punting was included as a course recreation. Punts are photogenic and there are often calls for them for T.V., movies and advertising agencies. September can be one of the pleasantest times to take a punt on the river; it is quiet and empty. It is a time when at weekends one can sometimes find parties of the nostalgically minded, occasionally very elegantly dressed, or even in fancy dress, perhaps recalling their undergraduate days as if with thoughts expressed by a writer in *Cherwell* over twenty years ago: "Punting is suffering from the current Oxford folly of trying to live in the present. Like Oxford, punting should be treated as a retreat from reality," or by another later writer, "We enjoy our summer terms in Oxford... But the one single pleasure which delights the inward eye more than any other is the tender recollection of punting on the river."

The comparative spaciousness and remoteness of the water used for punting at Oxford, has made punting mainly a means of relaxation and rest and quiet. At Cambridge, with less river space and the most popular part of it placed publicly in college gardens, punting is more often used as an opportunity for fun and amusement. The different natures of the rivers may encourage different uses. At Oxford, pole-snatching is by custom not practised, and all the bridges on the water usually punted on are too high for pole-picking.

The stretches of river punted on at Oxford can be considered in three parts: the Upper Cherwell above Parson's Pleasure, with the Cherwell Boat House at Bardwell Road at about the centre of it; the Lower Cherwell from Parson's Pleasure to the Isis, with Howard at Magdalen Bridge at about the centre of it; the Isis, with Hubbucks (and Fisher with glass-fibre punts) at Folly Bridge at the upper end of it – though many punts from Folly Bridge head for the Cherwell.

The Upper Cherwell is on the whole deeper and muddier than other stretches of river, as should be expected above a weir. However, the Cherwell Boat House serves North Oxford, the fashionable part of the town, and it is popular particularly for that reason. It has about 80 punts, with two or three 2ft 3in or 2ft punts. Its prices always used to be slightly more than at other boat houses, except in the last two years when they have been slightly less. The boat house provides no service as it would be understood by boat-hirers. Hirers find and return their own cushions, poles and paddles and are charged for the time doing it, something of a disadvantage to the incompetent or slow. The practice may have followed from undergraduates using college punts in block-bookings, preferring to do things for themselves.

The river both upstream and downstream is very beautiful. When the stream is slack it is not always immediately apparent at the Cherwell Boat House which way the stream is flowing. As you face the river, upstream is to the left and downstream to the right. Downstream, on the right bank, is first the playing field of the Dragon (boys' preparatory) School; then the gardens of Lady Margaret Hall, where the river passes through a bend; and finally the exceptionally beautiful University Parks. The water here is perhaps the most beautiful in Oxford and the beauty more natural than the Backs at Cambridge. Half way down is the concrete Rainbow Bridge, built in 1923, from funds collected by the mayor to provide unemployment relief. There are wooden palings across the river at Parsons' Pleasure; punts may go through them to the rollers. Just before Parsons' Pleasure, below a low bridge straight ahead, is a millstream cut called New College backwater, very shallow and overgrown. It goes down to St Catherine's College boat house and a weir.

Upstream from the Cherwell Boat House there is almost immediately the foot bridge crossing from Wolfson College to fields belonging mainly to the Oxford Preservation Trust, and beside it Wolfson College with its own punt-harbour. Beyond this is a bend where on the open side of the river the prevailing crosswind can often make steering difficult for a punt for thirty of forty yards. A long, straight reach then goes up to Marston Ferry Road bridge. The bridge can be punted under, if the pole is not brought to the vertical. Just beyond this are the extensive grounds and landing places of the Victoria Arms, on the left bank, to the right. This is often the goal of undergraduate punters, the traditional place to go for a drink. It is the site of Marston Ferry, a rope punt-ferry that had existed for 600 years until recently; the old ferry is now in the car park, planted with flowers. Beyond the Victoria Arms, the river used to be maintained as private; but is now punted on. It passes the grounds of Summer fields, a private school; the waterside houses of Summertown; Cromwell's Meadow, an island (the name's origin is unknown but it may date from the Civil War); the Cherwell Hotel and on to the Northern Bypass bridge; then on several miles to Water Eaton and Islip. A map is useful when punting beyond the bridge. The punt-hirer at Magdalen Bridge, at the centre of the Lower Cherwell is Howard. The landing-stage is down a slope on the college side of the bridge. The punts are kept well below the bridge and brought up as required. The service is good. Almost the whole of the Lower Cherwell is reasonably shallow, especially below

51

the rollers at its upper end. This part of the river is not so beautiful, lacking vistas, but is popular because the bottom is good. It is useful to know the main stream, because it divides, but it does not take long to find out if you are on the wrong stream. At Magdalen Bridge there is only one stream to follow up river, the one to the right, on the far side. Below Magdalen Bridge, the river is beautiful, passing the Botanic Gardens and Christ Church Meadows. A little below the bridge, the river divides to go round an island. The branch to the right, along Christ Church Meadows is narrower and more overgrown. To the left, the river goes under a low footbridge. It turns to the right to follow St Hilda's College gardens, along a reach with an excellent bottom. (The turn to the left, under the road bridge, is blocked after some distance.) The two streams join again, just above a wire punt-ferry used by Christ Church men crossing to their playing fields. The river follows a walled bank along Christ Church Meadows to the end of a long reach and there divides. The main stream, the New Cut, is to the left and with a good bottom, reaches the Isis, the main stream of the Thames. The fork to the right is the old mouth of the Cherwell; it is narrow, devious, muddy and overgrown, but shallow. A punt with a Thames Conservancy licence should be used, if going on the Isis.

From Folly Bridge, downstream, the river is not as deep as it looks and has a good bottom. It is better on the towpath side. The first footbridge on the left is over the old mouth of the Cherwell; it is worth exploring the old mouth if you wish to leave the Isis and cross to the main stream of the Cherwell. The main mouth of the Cherwell is at the end of the college boat houses. There is a deep hole in the Isis near this mouth, but it is gradually filling in; if you find it, paddle with your pole and you will soon pass it. Beyond, is a long journey down to Iffley, through the bend known as the Gut and under Donnington

Road bridge. Iffley and Iffley lock are at the end of the reach; it has rollers also, but it is preferable to go through the lock and paddle with the pole where the river is too deep. A punt over 20 years old risks damage going over rollers. During the summer term, the Isis is rowed on by eight-oared boats and sometimes uncoxed boats. Punts should try to keep clear of them. It is better to follow the bank when there are eights on the river. At Folly Bridge is Hubbucks, with rafts under and above it. The entrance is from the old toll-house at the St Aldate's end. Hubbucks has a variety of punts, about fifty in all, mainly traditional Thames punts. Hubbucks is always prepared to let camping punts, provide them for special purposes or deal in punts or private repairing.

Below Folly Bridge, behind the Head of the River public house is G.M. Fisher, of Ware. Fisher planned to open a boat-hire business on British Waterways water in Hertfordshire. Negotiations were unsuccessful; but he had meanwhile found twelve of Scudamore's Thames punts at Cambridge for sale made surplus by the introduction at Cambridge of Camford punts. He looked for a hiring stage on the Cam, but found the river already too crowded. He therefore looked for a site in Oxford. A new public house, The Head of the River, was opening in Salter's former boat house below Folly Bridge and was prepared to lease him a landing stage. In 1978, he brought the twelve Scudamore Thames punts to Oxford; at the end of the season, they were washed downstream and ten of them were lost. He replaced them with ten Salter's glass-fibre punts. Though they are not traditional Thames punts, the position of the landing-stage below the bridge probably makes their hire more attractive for beginners, because they do not have to pass under the bridge, as they do from Hubbucks's rafts.

# Techniques of Punting

THE FIRST PART of this chapter deals historically with the punting stroke, giving descriptions of it published between 1898 and 1960, with additions by R.C. Bending on training for punt racing and by Tony Christie on the bucket recovery. The second part deals with the stroke for beginners and for pleasure and racing punters, under different headings, and ends with advice on safety in punting and on the rule of the road; this part has been revised by, and includes a section by Penny Chuter, senior national rowing coach for Britain.

An early, but one of the most useful and thoughtful accounts of punting is given in Leslie's *Our River*. The more important parts of it are reproduced in Chapter 2. Though Leslie's was a fishing punt, his is the advice of an excellent waterman, and it deserves careful study by both experienced and inexperienced waterman.

In *Pleasure and Leisure Boating* (1899), Sydney Crossley includes a chapter on punting. His description is of running, not pricking a punt, and unlike other authors he has no interest in punt racing. He states three first principles for the learner: "1. Keep the pole parallel to the

side, 2. Push in the exact opposite direction to that in which you want
the punt to go, 3. Keep the pole out of the boat and your hands dry."
Next he advises the beginner not to begin by using the pole, but to find
a walled bank or some camp-shedding, to stand at the bow facing the
stern, and to move the punt using the fingers. By this means, the learner
will find how much effort is needed to change the direction of the punt
and how it is applied with the fingers. The advice is excellent: for very
little effort and change of direction is required to steer a punt, and
movement of the fingers and forearms needed to move the punt along
the wall is almost identical to their movement when using the pole. As
a result the principle of punting with the fingers would be understood
and experienced and established very early. Indeed, the pole planted
parallel to the side might be considered as the wall, with a very slight
angle in or out to steer. The fault of the novice, Crossley surmises, is to
use too much effort: "He steps forward and makes a plunge with the
iron (shoe)... His impetuosity is so great as nearly to send him over the
side..." Crossley expects the punter to give constant thought to his task,
and having written an earlier chapter on rowing, he concludes, "In point
of science and recreation, punting beats rowing hollow." Like Leslie, he
has a high regard for Maidenhead punts: "...all the best punts come
from Maidenhead ... the best Maidenhead punts are shoved lighter,
keep their 'way' better, hold themselves stiffer, and last longer than those
built elsewhere." The punting stroke is described in each of the four
books on punting and in later articles from journals or chapters from
books. The first book on punting, *Rowing/Punting* (a double volume)
by D.H. McLean & W.H. Grenfell (1898), is a reprint of Grenfell's
article on punting in *The Suffolk Encyclopaedia of Sport* (1897/8). Grenfell
gives good general advice on punting, Beesley's surname is misspelt
throughout, though the coach is greatly praised by Grenfell, his pupil.

55

There are four photographs of Grenfell demonstrating the stroke, on dry land in a studio. His hands are at least 12in apart for the shove, and for the finish even more than this, perhaps from unfortunate posing. He includes a useful description of how to run a punt, giving it as the style of Edward Andrews; it is reprinted in Chapter 2, and its study is recommended to all interested in watermanship.

Grenfell's description of the stroke is as follows:

"A good punter should be able to punt either side equally well; but supposing that you are punting with the right hand leading, place your right foot firmly against a knee of the boat, or some other well-defined spot, where she balances the best, and keep it there. Fix your eyes on the bow of the punt right through the stroke, and do not let them come round with the pole, or you will lose your direction, and a punt should never be allowed to deviate a hairsbreadth from the true course. If the punt is going fast, drop in the pole well in front of you (the distance depends in a great degree on the depth of the river and the pace at which you are going), raise your hands as far up the pole as you can, get the weight well on, keeping the pole quite close to the chest, and finish with the weight on and the chest square. Then recover the pole smartly with the hands, draw the extended foot gently back, so as not to shake the punt, and commence the next stroke. The work should be done with the weight, loins, and legs, and not with the arms. In fact it is not unlike rowing. You reach forward to the full extent, apply the weight then take a step back which corresponds to sliding, finish square, and, as it were, slide slowly forward and repeat the dose. The long body swing, smart recovery with the hands, and slow sliding forward will always beat the snatchy armwork which is the pitfall of racing punts."

The second book, also *Rowing/Punting* (another double volume) by R.R.P. Rowe, C.M. Pitman & P.W. Squire (also 1898), was published in the Badminton Library of Sport. The author of Punting is P.W. Squire. He gives a full description of the stroke with the photographic illustrations of W. Haines, then professional champion. Whereas Grenfell's hands were at least a foot apart on the pole, Squire recommends six inches. His description is this:

"The pupil should practise punting on both sides; but we will assume that he will begin with his right leg forward, and will stand on the left side of the punt. The right foot should be placed in a position where it is not likely to slip; in light racing-punts special stops are fixed for the forward foot to rest against, but in the larger punts one of the 'knees' is used for this purpose."

"For starting a punt, the iron end of the pole is dropped in the water just behind the left foot, while the hands should grasp the pole rather higher up than the level of the punter's head, and the arms be extended well forward towards the head of the punt. In this position the pole will be as much slanted, and the punt should start as soon as the pull of the stroke begins. The reach of the left arm is much increased by bringing the left shoulder round and raising the left heel. Most of the weight of the body should be supported on the front or right leg, the balance of the body being assisted by the left leg resting on the toes of the left foot. The left shoulder is brought more round to get the catch at the beginning with the left hand, which is a very important feature of the punting stroke. In that position the right hand cannot reach the pole above the left, but it is held ready to catch on as soon as possible. There should be a space of about six inches between the hands, and as the punt moves forward the right hand can take up its proper position on the pole; the work is then done by both hands equally. The right knee is slightly bent, and this position assists the balance. When the pull has brought the hands to the body, the latter turns on the spine as an axis, and in the turn the stroke is completed by the sway of the body on to the left leg, and by pushing the hands away towards the stern of the punt. The left arm should finish about straight. The hands should pass with an even, uninterrupted motion, from the beginning of the stroke to the end, and the pressure on the pole should be continuous throughout. During the pull of the stroke the back foot travels over the floor of the punt, and comes to rest on it as the hands reach the body; the latter then turns, and when completing the stroke by pushing the arms out to their full extent, the left knee bends so as to allow the whole force to continue to the end. Without this bend of the knee the stroke is short and loses much of the power of what has been called the 'after shove' and 'back shove'.

"Picking up the pole in the recovery for the next stroke is by no means an unimportant part of punting. Immediately after the stroke is finished the right hand should draw the pole through the left to a certain distance, which will in each case depend upon the depth of the water and consequent length of the pole which has been used; the left hand will then throw the pole over the right, which in turn will catch it and the action will be completed by the right hand lifting the pole clear of the water in a vertical position, the left taking hold of it in its passage, and helping to support it until returned to the water. Having arrived at this position, the pole is not merely dropped into the water, but sent down sharply to avoid loss of time; it is allowed to pass freely through the left hand, which should at the same time be raised, bringing the left shoulder round to get as much reach forward as possible. This completes the description of the punting stroke as it should be practised."

B.H.B. Symons-Jeune published *The Art of Punting* privately in 1907, at the time when punting had reached its greatest popularity. The title of his book would be unacceptable today; for oarsmen, rowing is a technique, not an art, and so are the other skills of watermanship. Symons-Jeune stresses the importance of the stroke being made as a continuous action, and recommends counting to ensure there is no break in the swing. He describes the stroke thus, making three divisions for it:

"At the commencement of the stroke (Division I) the pole is sent down into the water with a rapid throw, in which the right hand passes the left, which at the same time is lifted upwards to grasp the pole in front of the body. The pole should strike the water well in front of the front foot according to the rate the punt is travelling: from three to four feet in a racing punt going down stream, to about six to eight inches in a heavy punt full of people going up stream. As the pole touches the bottom, the top of it is pointed well forward and upward and the centre cuts the water line about two inches behind the front foot. At this moment Division 2 commences by a pull begun by the left hand, while the right is passing upwards to assist in the stroke; as both hands come on to the pole they should be placed about two or three inches apart. It is a great mistake to have the hands too far apart, as it will interfere with the whole of the after-stroke. A very gentle play off the front toe will assist the punter to get his weight well on, and as this is applied the end of the pole should be slightly dropped, to allow the hands to pass across parallel and close to the chest, which swings round with the stroke. Meanwhile the hind foot should pass back over the floor of the punt as low as possible to it to a distance of two treads, or, in the case of a big man, two-and-a-half. If the step be longer than this it will be difficult to recover, and must jerk the punt. The back knee should be bent a little as it touches the ground, and when the pole comes round the weight is mainly transferred from the front leg to the back, which slowly pivots round on the ball of the foot until the toe points to the stern. The leg should move back in conjunction with the hands, but not before them, and as the hands reach the body they should be held close to the chest, while the latter swings round till it faces the stern. Up to this point the stroke has been a pull, and now it immerges gradually into a push. As the body turns round, both hands together should be thrust away with a push into which all the muscles of the chest as well as of the arms are put. It is this last extra shove which makes all the difference in the force of the stroke, for it occurs after the weight has been used, and when the punt is travelling at its fastest.

"As soon as the arms are extended to their fullest extent the recovery (Division 3 of the stroke) begins without the slightest pause. Both hands should draw in the pole until they are nearly level with the chest, and at that moment the back leg should swing up close to the front one and both should assume an erect position. The leg and the pole should swing up together as the motion of the former will lighten the exertion of lifting the pole, and ease the arms to a great degree.

"As to the motion of the hands in making the recovery, there are two ways; the first and usual way at present, though not the best is as follows. The pole after being drawn in slightly before the movement of the leg, is pulled by the right hand through the left and then brought forward by the left while the right hand presses underneath to hold it; this necessitates a change of hands and causes the weight of the pole to come more on the arms, which imparts a slight jerk between the throws of the pole from one hand to another.

"The modern way does away with this: the pole is passed from hand to hand by the right hand pulling it through the fingers of the left as far as is comfortable, when the left hand glides up the pole until close to the right, and so on until the pole is in an erect position; thus the hands never cross as in the previous method, and the pole is recovered in a much more slanting position and seems to swing up almost with the motion of the body."

Symons-Jeune recommends a distance of two to three inches between the hands on the pole. The recommended distance had been decreasing from Grenfell's to Squire's to Symons-Jeune's. In the modern racing stroke the hands are as close together on the pole as the hands on a golf club.

His description of the alternative or "modern" (as he calls it) method of picking up is interesting. The method was certainly not subsequently established in racing. It may have been a method of recovery seen used in Oxford for what is described later in this chapter as "punting with hands low." The conventional punting stroke was taught and used in Oxford; but in the 1890's there was certainly a style of punting, a vogue perhaps, possibly an Oxford idiosyncrasy, rather different in purpose, to achieve maximum relaxation, the body upright and making as little movement as possible. The idiosyncrasy may be of some historic interest. The technique perfected, it will be found no more difficult to punt sitting down than standing up (though that was not its purpose). I have taken the term "punting with hands low" from G.D. Leslie's advice to a novice learning to keep dry, "as soon as he learns to keep his hands low in working, the drips will no longer trouble him."

Symons-Jeune has a brief, useful chapter on steering; this advises against use of the swing: "A method often seen on the river for steering purposes is to take the end of the pole in both hands and swing it through the top of the water in either direction at the back of the punt... This is never to be recommended, and is never employed by good watermen to steer with, for it has several serious disadvantages." He then surmises obvious mechanical inefficiencies of it. He recognises the difference of effort required in steering a racing punt and a pleasure punt: "It is much easier to steer a racing punt and a two-foot than an ordinary punt, as the lightness of the vessel makes it answer much more quickly to every touch. Owing to the great weight of a heavy punt, it takes an effort to straighten it, and when once on the swing it is difficult to stop." He notes a change in style in the turning of the body: "A few years ago it was a golden rule never to take the eyes off the bow of the punt at any part of the stroke, as it enabled one to keep a straight course more easily. But now several expert punters turn their heads right round with their bodies; and there is no doubt that this enables them to get in a much longer back-shove with more strength to it."

Symons-Jeune's own interest was centred squarely in punt racing. He viewed pleasure punting perhaps with some disdain: "so many people think it is a sign of good punting to keep dry and not to splash the punt with water, and it is of course very useful for ladies punting for pleasure; but this can only be done by punting carefully and slowly, and it is absolutely impossible when travelling fast. In a race, for instance, everyone gets dripping, and very often an inch of water has to be baled out afterwards." He overstates the difficulty of keeping a punt dry when punting at pressure; for although in racing, a very fast recovery is a cause of wetness, it is possible in a pleasure punt to use a good deal of pace and pressure and to keep perfectly dry. Punting for pleasure, it was common at less pressure to use a comfortable and easy continuous half-shove.

Though an Oxford man, Symons-Jeune advised standing behind the after back-rest to punt, forward of the till: "When carrying passengers, the punter should stand in the stern of the punt with his front foot placed against the 'knee' of the punt, just behind the back of the seat. This will allow him room enough to step well back in his stroke, whereas if he stands in the bows, the slope of the punt will render his position less secure." There is, in fact, no difference of slope for either position when standing immediately behind a back-rest, whether punting bow first or stern first (from the Oxford end). Perhaps he wished to emphasise the orthodoxy on the Thames of punting bow first. There would of course have been no question of standing on the till; it would have been regarded as a misuse of the punt.

An article in *Every Woman's Encyclopaedia* (about 1908 – the British Library catalogue does not have it) gives advice for punting. Some of it is taken verbatim from Squire and Grenfell, well selected and arranged in numbered items. "It is very important to acquire a good style in punting from the outset, for when once this is fixed, it is almost impossible to alter it... I. when punting alone in the boat, stand almost in the middle of the punt, close to the right hand side, in order to make a slight keel by means of your weight. 2. Punt on the right-hand side of the boat, at least while learning, because this enables you to get the first pull on the pole with the right hand and arm — almost always considerably stronger in a woman — and when the art of punting on that side has been mastered, by all means practise punting from the left-hand side also, for to be able to punt from either side is often a great advantage, especially for punt racing at regattas. 3. Keep the hands quite close to each other on the pole, and never move them from their first position throughout the stroke. When turning the punt, the hands are placed a couple of feet apart, instead of within about six inches of each other. 4. *Steer entirely by means of the pole on the bottom of the river.* Never steer with the pole in the water behind the boat as though it were a rudder. 5. Pick up the pole with three clean-cut movements, never draw it up hand over hand. 6. Return the pole to the water with a single throw." The instructions are well expressed; but right-handed punt racers prefer to stand on the left side.

There are good descriptions of the punting stroke in *Punting* by A.M. Winstanley (1922). He gives a long and detailed description of the stroke and concludes with the brief summary quoted later; this summary is as useful as his longer description. The introduction to Winstanley's *Punting* (1922) was written by Lord Desborough (W.H. Grenfell). In this introduction, Lord Desborough described the punting stroke briefly and very effectively understood by any oarsman. He compared it, as other writers had done, to the rowing stroke: "In punting, as in rowing, you should (1) come slowly forward with the body; (2) reach well up the pole and get your weight on to the beginning; (3) swing well back, using the free leg like a sliding seat; (4) finish the stroke well out, turning the body from the hips, but not letting it tumble forward; (5) recover the pole sharply with the hands; and (6) slide, as it were, slowly forward again by bringing up the disengaged leg without shaking the punt."

In 1926, in *The Civil Service Sports Journal*, A.E. Banham wrote an article on punting. His description of the punting stroke, except for the pick up or recovery, is very lucid: "Stand at the side of the punt, not facing forward, but with the shoulders just about 'square', i.e., parallel, to the river bank. The head only should be turned forward. We will suppose that the punter is standing on the left side of the punt, as one looks forward. The left hand at the height of the waist holds the pole in an almost vertical position. The right hand at a height a little above the head steadies the pole. The pole is then thrown down smartly with the right hand so that its shoe rests on the bottom of the river, the left hand comes up to the full extent of the arm and catches the pole, the weight of the body is hung on the pole and the right hand comes up and grips the pole above and touching the left. The stroke has now commenced. The pull on the pole by means of the arms changes smoothly into a push as the hands pass exactly across the middle of the chest and the right shoulder comes on to the work. The stroke is carried right through and finishes with hands well behind. It is the last part of the stroke – known as the backshove – that the untrained punter usually omits... The pectoral muscles have to be developed a bit by practice if the stroke is to pass in one strong unbroken movement from the natural pull with which it commences into a rearward shove." Banham adds, "Don't stand on the counter (or deck) of the punt. It is impossible to punt properly there, and none of the real punting fraternity ever does it."

Banham gives advice on steering: "When the beginner comes to steer he should remember that steering should not be done by trailing the pole behind and using it as a rudder. This spoils poles and wastes time. Steering is all done in the stroke and it is done thus. To steer to the left, simply draw the hands inboard a little during the latter part of the shove, the pole being levered against the side of the punt ... it is obvious that if you lever or 'pinch' the after-end to the right, the fore-end will swing to the left.

"Steering to the right is as difficult to learn as steering to the left is easy... get the punt moving and during the latter part of the stroke lean out and bring the punt towards the pole by a combined use of the arms, weight and (in imagination perhaps) toes."

He concludes with a succinct description of racing, "A punting race finishes where it starts and usually consists of ¼ mile each way, the turning point being marked by poles standing up in the river, known as 'ryepecks'. A punt is reversible like a tramcar, and the turn is accomplished by dropping the pole far forward, bringing the punt to a dead stop, and steering the stern which has now become the bow, round the ryepeck as the punt starts on the return journey... Punt races start downstream, the turn is toward the bank and the finish is, of course, up-stream." It is more usual to recommend the steering for the turn as the punt first passes the ryepeck, passing from one side to the other behind the pole before the stop-up is made; the turn is then completed as the stop-up finishes, and the punt is pointing straight forwards towards to the finish as it repasses the ryepeck coming up-stream. Punt races are almost always started downstream because the direction of the stream holds them straighter for the start than if started upstream. The course usually taken is the midstream side going downstream, to use the current, and the bank-side to avoid it coming up; therefore the turn is usually made towards the bank. Punters on the whole prefer to make the turn against the stream, from downstream to upstream.

In 1929, Giles gave instructions on the menu card for Lyons tea shops as do's and don'ts. Among his do's and don'ts he said: "Do not try to use a long, heavy pole — a 13ft pole is quite long enough for most reaches on the Thames. It should not be so big that you cannot get your hand comfortably around it. If you want to improve your punting, go out alone and stand in the middle of the punt. In that position, you will be far less affected by cross-winds and much less likely to oversteer. Do not try to steer by waving the pole about in the water behind the punt. When steering is necessary, put the pole into the water, sloping either towards you or away from you and either push the punt slightly away or pull it towards the pole as you push the punt along. "Do not stand on the counter or decked-in part at the stern of the punt. Apart from being quite incorrect, this is one of the most difficult places from which to punt. Always make sure that the pole has touched the bottom of the river before you push on it. This may sound silly, but carelessness in this respect is the usual cause of people falling in. If your pole sticks in the mud, it is far safer to let go, and then paddle back and fetch it. If you try to hang on, it will probably pull you into the water." The Thames Punting Club regatta programme for 1949 included a short article on punting. For the punting stroke, it gave the following advice.

"The first golden rule of punting is, *Never move the foot nearest the bow.*
It should be securely wedged against one of the 'knees', with the foot
at an angle of approximately 60 degrees to the side of the punt. (The
knees are the small wooden struts fastened along each side.) "Next in
importance is always, at the commencement of each new stroke, to
stand erect, with heels together, and body and head facing forward.
Reach high up the pole with the rear hand, and immediately the pole
has touched the bed of the river place the other hand just above, grasp
firmly with both hands, lean forward, slope the top of the pole slightly
down to the bow, pull down and shove across the chest.

"Remember to keep head facing in the direction the boat is going –
it is not until the top of the pole is level with the punter that he should
swing round on his hips and face sideways. Meanwhile, the forward
foot remains stationary, takes the whole weight of the body and is
pressed forcibly against the bottom of the boat. The rear foot should
now be raised an inch and gently slid along the bottom and side of
the punt towards the stern. When the punter faces sideways, but not
before, the rear foot is brought firmly to rest on the bottom of the boat
and the weight is transferred to that foot.

"During the whole of the stroke the forward foot never moves, and the
two hands must maintain exactly the same position on the pole. Never
allow the hands to be parted whilst putting weight or pressure on the pole.
A continuous even pressure should be applied and maintained throughout
the stroke until the body has turned so far round that the pole is touching
the forward shoulder. At the completion of the stroke, the forward hand
draws – or gently swings – the pole up through the rear hand, the rear
hand forming a loose ring round the pole. Avoid splashing. At the same
time the rear foot should be brought up to the forward one. See that all
your actions are smooth: care must be taken not to 'rock' the boat.

"Whereas the bow and the stern should be approximately at the same level, it is a mistake to think that a punt must lie flat on the water. It should tilt along its whole length towards the side on which the punter stands. If, therefore, a passenger occupies the centre, that passenger should be at the opposite end, but on the same side, as the punter. Friction with the water will be minimised, and consequently less effort required to propel the punt.

"By sloping the pole, whilst it is on the bottom of the river, towards or away from the punt you either push the stern away from or draw it towards the pole, thus steering the punt in the required direction. Never try to lever the punt over against the pole: more poles are broken in this way than through any other cause. No punter should stand on the rear deck: punting should be performed from the well of the punt."

In 1953, Nevill Miroy wrote an article on punting for *The Light Blue*, a Cambridge sports magazine. His advice for the punting stroke was, "The would-be punter should take up his position about three-quarters of the way towards the stern of the craft on the port or starboard side, and let the pole slide through his hands until it just touches the bottom. The angle at which he starts this movement is judged so as to bring the underwater end of the pole just astern of him as it touches the bottom; therefore when the 'shove' is started, the pole is approximately at an angle of 45° to the bottom and to the punter. If his craft has 'way on', the punter thrusts the pole well forward to allow time for it to reach the bottom. He then thrusts astern with both arms, taking a step in the same direction with the rear foot. At the end of a stroke, he pulls the pole forward almost horizontally above the water, either gathering it in hand over hand, or by a sharp jerk throwing it forward so that it slides through his fingers. As it comes up, the lower end is brought forward ready to re-enter the water at the correct angle, and at the same moment the feet are brought neatly together.

"*Steering is probably the most difficult part of punting.* If a punter wants to steer his craft to the left while punting on the right, he puts his pole into the water a foot or so from the side of the boat, and, while making his stroke, draws the stern of the punt towards the pole, even allowing the pole to go slightly underneath the stern; but he must take care not to get the pole under the boat or he may be pulled out. If he wants to steer to the right, then during the stroke he pushes the stern slightly away from the pole. It is important not to get a 'swing' on the boat as this is difficult to stop."

In 1960, the EP Publishing Group added to its series of booklets on sports the title *Know the Game: Boating*, now out of print. It had three sections: on sculling, canoeing and punting. The section on punting was written by R.C. Bending, T.P.C. champion from 1946–49. As a keen amateur photographer, Bending took photographs of punting for it; an artist then made line drawings of them for the illustrations in the book. For a punter standing on the left of the punt, his instructions for the stroke were: "Stand in the punt with your right foot close to the side and at an angle of 45°. Face square forward and hold the pole with your right hand at the distance of your own height from the shoe of the pole; your left hand holds it loosely about three feet below. Throw the pole down with your right hand and follow it down letting it slide through your fingers. Simultaneously reach well up and forward with your left hand and as soon as the pole hits the bottom, grip it with your left hand and start to pull. As soon as you start to pull with your left hand, reach up with your other hand and grip the pole above the left hand. Your rear foot will automatically lift a little as your right hand reaches up. Pull both hands in towards your chest and at the same time slide your rear foot backwards about two feet, depending on the length of your leg and the amount of effort being put into the stroke. Your front knee may bend slightly and the weight of your body should come on to the pole. Now turn your trunk round and begin to bend your rear knee. Continue to swing your trunk round, at the same time shooting your hands out towards the rear, and continue to bend your rear knee in a lunging movement. The recovery can be done in a leisurely manner. Grip the pole with your right hand and pull it through the left hand, at the same time turning your trunk towards the front. When punting in deep water it is advisable to spread your arms well out. Then grip the pole with your left hand and continue to move it up. Move your right hand backwards down the pole and grip it at a point about your own height from the bottom. (For punting with a long pole in deep water it may be necessary to repeat the movements to bring the pole clear of the water.)" By this Bending is advising a pick up in five: the pick up should always be made in an odd number of movements, whether in one — the bucket — or in three, or in more. "Move your right hand, which is now gripping the pole, up and forwards and continue to swing your body round towards the front. Draw the pole through your left hand until your hands are about three feet apart. Your weight will now be over your front foot and the other foot is drawn smoothly towards it. At the same time bring the pole towards the upright position. Continue to move your body round until it is facing square forward and bring the pole ready into the first position." His special advice on steering is: "Only steer *half* the angle you wish to turn, the swing of the punt will look after the rest."

Bending's instructions do not seem to make clear enough the importance of the control of the pole with the rear hand of the forward and lateral angles as it moves to the upright position for the drop when he says, "the left hand holds it (the pole) loosely": the hand should be relaxed, but its movement and control at this point decide precisely the place and angle for the drop of the pole. Bending's instructions were based on his racing stroke with modifications to reduce its pressure for pleasure punting. Bending, regarded as an exceptionally good stylist, said however that when racing he punted standing virtually on one foot. Though the rear foot moved back and forward for the after-shove, it hardly touched the punt; the body recovered its position at the end of the shove from its weight on the pole, not the foot. That Bending appeared to stand only on one foot when racing is confirmed by those who watched him.

Notes provided by R.C. Bending on training for punt racing include this advice: "I. Get a good coach. 2. Develop a good style. 3. Do most of your long distance early in the season so that your style gets well established. 4. Get out in all conditions. Learn to handle the punt when a half gale is blowing. 5. Get to know the course. 6. Never waste time at the ryepeck. When turning move across the ryepeck as you pass it, so that when you stop up and reverse, your course is then directly ahead. Pass as closely as possible. 7. Practise dropping the pole and picking up the spare without losing rhythm. Picking up the pole on the same side can be done without any check, but also practise picking up the pole on the opposite side without a check. 8. Follow down the throw with the hand. This will cope with any pot holes. 9. Do not use a pole longer than necessary for the course."

Punt racers have always believed that a large proportion of races are won or lost at ryepecks. A punter picks up the spare pole with almost the same movement as the recovery, moving lower for it, so to the unobservant watcher a pole left behind may appear in the river as if from nowhere; with the hands relaxing at the end of the stroke, a pole sticking is left by the momentum of the punt.

This description of the bucket recovery is provided by Tony Christie, T.P.C. champion for 1961–3. "The shove through the water right up to the finish of the stroke is the normal power transmission. It is at the point of recovery that the variation arises. The forward hand draws the pole through the rear hand and the body turns towards the bow, both in one movement. The rear hand checks its forward momentum as the forward hand raises the pole ready for the downward throw for the next stroke. The forward hand throws the pole down, and the rear hand now above head height checks the pole as it strikes the bottom, holding it momentarily as the forward hand reaches above the rear hand and the stroke begins. The bucket, a forward movement in one, is far the fastest recovery, comparable to the hands away and forward movement on the slide of a best and best sculling boat." By comparison with the stroke with the pick up in three, the finish for the stroke with the bucket recovery is often made high, the stroke shorter and with a higher striking rate. Among racing punters in 1982, there is a tendency not to move the rear foot, which mechanically cannot be so efficient as when the foot is moved well to give a longer stroke. Before the introduction of the bucket, the word "throw" was always used for second movement of the recovery in the pick up in three, the forward throw of the pole by the rear hand. In modern punt racing, with the pick up in one, the word "throw" is not needed in describing the recovery, and it is often used now to describe what was formerly called the drop, the throw of the pole with the forward hand down to the river-bottom.

The side preference in punting is estimated at about 60–65% on the left and 35–30% on the right. Punters should learn on both sides early, because if one side only is learnt in the early stages it is very difficult to learn on the other side.

The foregoing descriptions of the punting stroke provide a historical account of it. The following descriptions are for those immediately concerned with the practice of punting.

## Paddling a Punt with Canoe Paddles

Paddling a punt is a pleasant alternative to punting it, with either double paddles or single. Using two paddles, the paddlers sit side by side on the till, with a back-rest cushion for a seat. Steering is done by increasing or reducing pressure on one side or the other. For paddling a punt with a single paddle, the stroke has technical similarities to the punting stroke. A racing punt carries no paddle, and if it must be paddled, it is done with the pole.

## Paddling a Punt with a Pole or Paddle

The stroke for a single paddle in a punt is the same as the stroke in a Canadian canoe.

A description of the stroke for the Canadian canoe follows, but a comparison with the punting stroke is included with it. It is even more relevant than the comparison with the rowing stroke. The difference, as with rowing, is that the paddle is forced against the water and the pole against the river bottom. Anyone who is competent in using a single canoe paddle and has not punted, will soon find himself able to punt after a short distance, if he will first propel the punt using the pole with the stroke of a single canoe paddle. The steering of a canoe with a paddle and a punt with a pole is almost identical.

To steer a canoe with a single paddle away from the side the paddler is paddling on, dip the paddle into the water (at a right angle to the side) a little away from the canoe; then towards the end of the stroke, turn the blade inwards, pulling it in towards the canoe. This effectively draws the stern towards the paddle and thus turns the bow away. To steer towards the side the paddler is paddling on, put the paddle in close to the canoe; then towards the end of the stroke, turn the blade outwards, pushing it away from the canoe (or if the blade is well under the canoe, lever it against the side). This is called the "J" stroke by canoeists and in effect it levers the stern away from the paddle, effectively turning the bow towards the "paddling" side. So also when a punt is steered from anywhere astern of the centre, direction is changed by pushing the stern, not the bow, away from or towards the pole. When running a punt from the bow, it is of course the direction of the bow that must be changed. The mechanics of steering a punt are exactly the same as steering a canoe, except that the pole is first thrown (or dropped) to the bottom. The former movement is the equivalent of "shoving around" and the latter of "pinching" the punt; a canoe was once also said to be "pinched".

If the experienced canoeist, while standing, learns to paddle with the lower part of the punt pole and steers as if with a single canoe paddle, he can then progress by throwing the pole down instead of dipping it, and will find he begins punting with the proper mechanical technique almost immediately, based on the single paddle stroke.

A pleasure punter should be able to paddle well with his pole; it is necessary in deep water and very useful over mud, so he should learn and practise it. Besides using a pole like a single canoe paddle, a punter, standing, can hold the pole horizontally across the punt like a double (kayak) canoe paddle, to paddle, dipping on alternate sides. Though requiring more effort than punting, a good speed can be maintained with either stroke when the punt has momentum.

Always take a canoe paddle in a punt in case you drop the pole and need to recover it. Some punt-hirers now provide paddles too small to allow good paddling. Ask for a large paddle if you intend to use it for more than this.

A competent punter with good balance may find enjoyment in punting a Canadian canoe. It can also be useful practice for punt racing. Lacking the weight of a punt, however, its movement will also lack the smoothness and momentum of a punt. Some regattas have canoe punting races. The major trophy is the Dardier Cup at the Sunbury Regatta.

## *The Punting Stroke*

Skill in rowing or punting is the achievement of maximum mechanical efficiency from physical effort; of maximum physical effort for full pressure and of minimum for light pressure. Pressure is determined by the length of stroke as well as by physical effort. In punting at full pressure, the pole comes to the vertical and if the punt is in deep water will be dropped ahead of the punter's forward foot. The full shove consists of two parts; the first, a pull on the pole as the hands are drawn towards the centre of the chest, the second a push when the hands pass it. The rear foot moves back with the push, to complete the "after shove" and comes forward again with the recovery. In punting, length of stroke can be reduced by using a "half-shove", dropping the pole at half the angle to the vertical, or 45°; or a ¾-shove, using three-quarters of the angle. When a punt is stationary or moving very slowly, it is necessary to use a half-shove to start it moving. A pleasure punt is heavy and its movement requires momentum. Until this is established, it is better to use half or three-quarter shoves, usually for the first three strokes.

A good punter should be able to punt from either side of the punt at any point along it from bow to stern. For racing, the forward foot is placed at, or just forward of, the centre point of the side against a "knee", and does not move from that position; also in a pleasure punt, but only as far forward as the saloon will allow. The nearer to the centre the punter stands, the less physical effort and movement required for steering during the stroke. In a pleasure punt, therefore, the punter should stand as far forward as the design of the punt allows. A racing punt is easier to steer than a pleasure punt, being lighter. If a beginner in a pleasure punt is improving and can take the opportunity to remove the saloon cushions and punt from there, it will assist in learning to steer during the stroke. A right-handed punt racer often prefers to stand on the left of the punt, so his right hand and foot are forward to begin the pull of the shove, the moment of greatest effort.

The punt will steer better if as much weight as possible, including that of the "sitters" or sitting passengers, is kept on the same side of the punt as the punter, thereby tilting the punt towards that side. This makes a shallow keel, helping to keep the punt straight. Both feet should be kept as near to the side as possible, with the forward foot pointing at an angle slightly forward and remaining stationary through-out the stroke.

In punting, the matter of greatest importance is posture. Almost every mistake follows from incorrect posture. The body must be relaxed and upright. Any bending of the back or crouching will cause inefficiency and possibly danger. Punting is a posture exercise, like rock-climbing, dancing or golf. Muscle tension of the rest of the body should never exceed that of the fingers. To maintain this rule may be a difficult discipline for a beginner, but it should be learnt. It is for this reason that with the stroke at fullest pressure, the hands cross the front of the chest as close to it as possible, while the body is relaxed and absolutely upright as the forward knee begins to bend.

The first and most important rule in punting therefore is to relax and keep upright. The beginner may feel that this is absurd, because thereby much less effort than is expected may be required, and the discovery may nonplus a beginner. However, keep two questions in mind. Can I stand even more upright? Can I make even more use of my fingers? When thinking about the movements of the stroke, keep your thoughts on the movement of your fingers; relaxing the rest of your, muscles, the rest of your movements will follow correctly. Stand upright and relax.

## Some Descriptions of the Punting Stroke

Four descriptions of punting follow for different stages of progress; first, for an absolute beginner lacking confidence; second, for the improver with pleasure punting in mind; third, for the beginner confident in handling a punt pole of any weight; finally a description by A.M. Winstanley of the old racing stroke with the recovery (or pick up) in three, before the introduction of the very light aluminium racing pole which made the pick up in one (the "bucket") the general practice in punt racing. One of the greatest stylists since the introduction of the bucket, punted in best and best punts virtually standing on only one foot all the time.

## For the Absolute Beginner

The absolute beginner is recommended to:

I. Stand near the end of the punt. If punting stern first, as at Oxford, stand at the top of the slope, or "swim"; if bow first, as at Cambridge, on the deck. If your balance is poor, you may stand with one foot away from the side; but as you gain confidence, be sure to bring it back to the side. Standing with one foot away from the side is less efficient mechanically and more dangerous when in difficulty. Many beginners do it, standing diagonally to the side because they feel safer. The stance becomes a habit and the faulty style is then difficult to change.

2. Use ½ or ¾ shoves, with ¾ as the maximum. This means, do not bring the pole upright. Throw it backwards and down with the forward hand, parallel and close to the side, with the lower hand to guide it, not to grip it. Do not check the pole when you have let it drop. It must fall uninterrupted all the way. Do not try to push it to the bottom, hand over hand. Wait until it touches. If it doesn't reach the bottom, recover it and try another half shove.

3. When the pole has reached the bottom, reach forward and pull the pole gently past your chest. The harder you pull, the more serious your steering errors will be.

4. When you have reached the end of your shove, relax your arms and the grip of your hands on the pole. (It is very important to develop this as a habit, because it ensures you do not fall in if the pole unexpectedly sticks.) Let the pole float to the surface, use it like a rudder, swinging it to one side or the other. Some beginners inexperienced in boats have difficulty in steering: the pole must be swung to the same side as the direction in which you wish to travel.

5. Recover the pole hand to hand until you can begin to tilt it. When it can tilt, tilt it half way and begin another half-shove. An absolute beginner may be helped by a passenger using a paddle, especially to help steer, but as little help as possible should be given, or the punter will not learn.

## For the Improver in a Pleasure Punt

### The Recovery
Much of the wetness to clothes and to punts is caused by not keeping the hands and pole over the water and by gripping the pole too hard

when recovering. The punt is a heavy craft and once it is moving the momentum will carry it for the distance given by two or three shoves. Therefore it is not necessary to recover early if you are not racing. The momentum of a punt is sufficient to pull a pole out of the bottom (except in mud, which you should be paddling over with your pole). It is unnecessary therefore to pull the pole out of the bottom. The pole is able to float of its own accord; it is unnecessary therefore to try to lift it or pull it from the water. Wait for it to float. If the pole is unvarnished and rough, allow time for water to run off it. You can hold the pole, floating astern with one finger of the forward hand if you wish; you can adjust the steering with a swing, if you wish, with a finger of the rear hand; no more effort is usually required, except in wind or a cross-stream. If you are punting for pleasure, this is another position in which to check your posture; relax and stand upright, with arms and hands low. Take a few moments to look at the river, to rest and to enjoy it.

The recovery should be made in an odd number of movements. The pick up in three is the usual. If you cannot pick up in three, pick up in five (or even seven). If you pick up in an even number, the control for angle will not come into the correct, the rear, hand, before the beginning of the next stroke. If you have an opportunity to use a pole on dry land, you can practise the pick up in three on a concrete, wood or gravel surface. It is a good movement to practise in this way because you can also ensure that you relax and keep upright at the same time. For the pick up in three, the forward hand, with an underhand grip, draws the pole forward. As it reaches its limit, the rear hand grips it overhand and throws it on. The forward hand grips it below and moves it forward to begin the tilt. The rear hand following below, forces the pole down and thereby moves it up to the vertical against the pressure from the now rigid forward arm. The rhythm of the pick up in three is long-short-long, and the sequence of movement is pole-body-foot.

*The Drop or Throw*

At the end of the recovery with the pole upright, the rear hand controls two nearly vertical angles; first, the angle of the tilt, forward or back, parallel to the side of the punt, altered for the depth of the water or the length of the stroke; secondly, the angle of the tilt sideways, used in steering. Both hands control the distance of the pole from the side. Concentrate on the control of the pole by the rear hand and perfect this. If the movement is not going well, keep the forward hand low. The lower the hands, the greater the control over the pole. If you are having difficulty dropping the pole at the right angle and place, keep the grip on the pole with the rear hand, held as low as possible, and use the forward hand to hold the pole lightly. When its position is correct, let the pole drop from the rear hand, following it with a light flick from the fingers of the forward hand or letting it slide through them. Do this until you have learnt control with the lower hand. Never check the fall of a pole. If it does not fall as you want, learn to control its position, concentrating on the use of the rear hand. Do not try to control its tilt forwards or sideways with the forward hand. Keep your fingers relaxed enough to feel the nature of the vibration as the pole strikes the bottom; it will always vary slightly and may tell you how to make your shove.

When the control of the pole has been mastered, so that it can be guided with perfect accuracy, it can be thrown with maximum effort by the forward hand (provided the river bottom is suitable). Penny Chuter describes the movement thus: "The correct movement should be compared with throwing a javelin, i.e., the arm is held straight behind the thrower and the power and trajectory of the javelin comes from the arm throwing from straight behind and across the body to straight in front and above the head; similarly, the pole is thrown directly into the water from reaching straight above the head until the arm is straight downwards."

When you are stationary, or moving slowly, remember that the pole must go into the water at an angle backwards. If you are stationary in shallow water, the angle should be at least 45°. This is called a half-shove. If you are moving slowly, the angle can be less. Establishing momentum in a pleasure punt usually requires three half-shoves.

### The Shove

Tighten your fingers enough at the beginning of the shove to make sure the shoe is firmly fixed in the river-bottom. This is the moment to check your posture; relax, straighten your body and as you begin to pull, for the first part of the shove, come to your most upright position with your body at its fullest height, drawing your hands towards you. This brings your hands close across the front of your chest. Turn and push away. Move your rear foot back, but do not bring your hands any lower than the descent made necessary by moving the foot. The back should be straight and the head up. If you are not certain of your direction or steering, resist putting weight on the beginning of the shove. Direction can be changed over the first foot or two of the shove, but not if you have shoved too hard and are travelling fast. At the end of the shove, the hands and fingers relax on the pole, if only momentarily. It is important to establish this relaxation as an unvarying habit. Again, when the fingers tighten to recover the pole, the tension, by habit, should never be so great as to pull the body backwards if the pole sticks. Leaving the pole behind if it has stuck too hard should be a reflex action. For the racing stroke, it is common to see the fingers stretch out on the pole before the recovery.

## Steering

Steering is part of the shove. The punt is steered by the angle at which the pole is thrown down. To steer away from the side you are facing, drop the pole so that its bottom is just outside the vertical line from the side of the punt to the river bottom and the top is a little further out still, making an inward slope with the pole a little away from the punt. Keeping as upright as possible, in spite of having to reach out, pull in towards you during the shove. This is "shoving around". To steer towards the side you are facing, throw down the pole close to the side you are facing and lean the pole inwards, so the top of the pole passes slightly over the side of the punt. This is called "pinching" the punt. With the precisely correct angle, the shove is made with both hands close together and the pole finishing straight astern.

With a heavy punt or a strong cross wind, when more strength is required, more leverage for steering can be obtained, using the same mechanical principle, by spreading the hands apart a little, usually by lowering the grip of the rear hand; then pushing outwards or pulling inwards with the lower hand during the stroke to move the stern towards you or away from you as you continue the shove, you will steer towards or away from the bank facing you. To steer away from the bank facing you ("shoving around"), the pole must be dropped well away from the side and pulled inwards. The wider apart the hands are, the more powerful will be the movement in steering.

The mechanical principle used in steering is to push the stern away or draw it in with the pole during the stroke. Using short sideways strokes of this kind, you can turn the punt in a complete circle either way without moving it forwards or backwards.

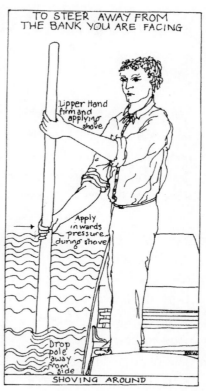

*Steering under difficulty.* When the pole is dropped with the correctly chosen lateral angle, no more need be done during the shove to move in the chosen direction. However, a reserve of mechanical force in steering a heavy punt in a cross–wind or in turning a sharp corner may be obtained by lowering the grip of the rear hand on the pole and pulling in or pushing out with it while making the shove, drawing the stern of the punt towards or pushing it away from the pole, thus turning the bow in the other direction. For "shoving around", forward pressure of the waist, knees and toes draws the stern of the punt towards the pole. For "pinching", the stern may be touched with the pole to turn it, but that is by no means essential.

## For the Beginner Confident in Handling a Punt Pole

This description of the punting stroke by Penny Chuter is valuable for beginners who are confident in handling a punt pole.

### The Recovery

Start with the pole "trailing" in the water at the end of a stroke with hands together on the pole.

The forward hand (under-hand grip) is nearest the top of the pole with the rear (over-hand grip) next to the forward hand and touching it. The pole is recovered by working the hands down hand-over-hand as follows. Grip pole with forward hand and pull it with forward hand up and across body with the rear hand holding loosely, and allow pole to be pulled through rear-hand fingers with right hand. When forward hand ahead of body, grip with the rear hand to stop pole moving and whilst gripping with rear hand, move the forward hand down pole crossing below rear hand. Then grip and support pole in forward hand and move rear hand down pole as far as possible. (If this "crossover recovery" does not get your hands far enough down the pole, then repeat the movement by crossing the forward hand below the rear hand again, etc.)

The hands will now be apart and ready to carry the pole forward for the next stroke. As the pole is moved forward and vertical, the rear foot also moves up closer to the forward foot.

### The Beginning (The Throw)

Just before the beginning, the weight is on the forward foot and the pole is held vertically in front of the body with the forward hand above the head and the rear hand holding it at about waist level. The pole is then thrown towards the bottom with the top (forward) hand throwing down and guiding the direction of the pole whilst simultaneously the lower hand is taken off the pole and moved up to grip the pole at maximum reach above the head. This hand immediately begins to pull as the forward hand, having thrown the pole down, then reaches up to grip the pole above (and touching) the other hand so that both are together on the pole. During the stroke the hands must be together on the pole (touching) so that the "reach" and "back-shove" equally share the pressure.

Normally the pole is thrown in vertically about I ft in front of the forward foot. If the water is deep, it should be angled about 20° forward. If very shallow, about 10° backwards.

### The Stroke

As both hands, and arms and shoulders, begin to pull downwards and towards the body, the rear foot steps back. As the hands are drawn across the body, the full weight is on the forward foot and the pole. As the hands pass across the body, the upper body turns with the pole and a strong back-shove is executed with the forward shoulder. As this is done, some body weight is transferred to the rear foot.

Remember the whole stroke is executed with hands together on the pole.

You are now ready to start the recovery again.

Practise the recovery movement with a broomstick at home or with a punt pole, standing on the bank. This will make your first effort afloat easier.

### Steering

Steering may be done in two ways:

A straight shove and steer with the pole.

A "C" shaped shove from out, to in, to out, to "pinch" the punt (or move to the pole-side of the punt); and a "C" shaped shove from in, to out, to in, to "shove around" (or move away from the pole-side).

## The Stroke at Full Pressure

Winstanley won the first Thames Punting Championship held after the 1914–1918 war. After a long description in his book of the punting stroke, he ends with a neat summary of it, reminiscent of the style of an army training manual, calling it "punting by numbers". (For everyday English, replace his full stops with "and" as appropriate.) He describes the stance, with the assumption that the left side is chosen when facing the bow: "The toes of the right foot should be against one of the 'knees' of the punt, and should never move from that position. The foot should form an angle with the side of the punt and not be straight across at right angles. The position of the left foot at the commencement of the stroke is close up to the right foot, and straight across the punt. The body should be upright but not stiff, and should be free on the hips and well balanced on the ankles. It is good practice in balancing, to stand in the position decribed and rock the punt by means of the ankles only."

Winstanley divides the stroke into lifting and dropping the pole:

"Lifting Pole. Left hand resting on pole, right hand underneath, feet together, right foot against a 'knee'. Hands close to side. (1) Right arm rises to the horizontal, right hand gripping pole. Left hand acts as slide. (2) Left hand grips pole. Right hand slides down pole until close to left. (3) Drop pole from left hand to right. (4) Right arm rises until is level with forehead and just in front of it, right hand gripping pole. Left hand reaches down pole, grips it and pushes it forward.

"Dropping Pole. (The Throw) (5) Pole allowed to drop while left hand slides up it to *full extent of arm*. Right hand follows pole down, fingers touching pole, until arm is extended fully downwards. Left hand must be well round pole. (6) When pole touches bottom, right hand raised and grips pole just above left hand. (7) Arms and body reach forward to give maximum angle on pole, at the same time left leg raised and moved back, foot not touching bottom. (8) Draw hands in towards chest, body kept facing well forward, *right knee gradually bending* (slightly only). (9) When hands are in to chest, turn body until facing square to stern, left foot touching bottom, and taking weight. (10) Arms shoot (or push) out towards stern, weight of body thrown backward on pole. (11) Recover body, arms and pole, and left foot until position I is assumed, hands keeping their position on the pole."

He adds:

"The hands should not drop below the level of the chest at the end of the shove unless, of course, the water is so deep as to necessitate this."

At full pressure, the shove is made with the hands close together on the pole, not moving till the shove is completed. Winstanley's is an excellent description of the old racing stroke, beginning with the pick up in three.

The illustrations on the next page are of the punting stroke at full pressure in a racing punt punted from the centre, but with a recovery or pick-up in three. The forward foot always remains stationary. The illustrations should be of help to a beginner confident in handling the pole easily; but before this, learn control of the pole in an upright and relaxing posture. The movements are of the classic punting stroke.

The illustrations were drawn from photographs especially taken for the purpose by R.C. Bending (T.P.C. Champion 1946–9). Bending developed a very full body turn for the racing stroke, and a pleasure punter may not turn so fully as shown in these diagrams.

*1. At the end of the shove, the hands, high and together, move away from the body to finish. The fingers relax on the pole and stretch out. (W10)*

*2. When the stroke has finished, the forward hand draws the pole forward, sliding it through the rear hand till the forward arm is almost horizontal.*

*The rear foot moves forward. (W1 & 11)*

*3. The rear hand grips the pole and throws it forward with a swing over the forward hand returning to catch it below at about the point of balance (W2 & 3)*

*4. The forward hand carries the pole forward, controlling its height; the rear hand controls its angles (fore-and-aft and lateral) pushing it forward and down to the position for the throw. (W4.i)*

*The punter is standing at the centre of a 2ft racing punt with a 12ft pole in about 3ft of water. The illustrations will be of help to a beginner who is confident in handling the pole easily. Before this, master control of the pole in an upright and relaxed position. Learn on dry land, if necessary.*

5. *The forward hand throws the pole down, its position precisely placed by the rear hand. (W4.ii)*

6. *As the pole reaches the bottom, the rear hand grips the pole high. (W5)*

7. *With the pole firmly in the bottom, the forward hand grips the pole closely above the rear hand; the pull of the hands towards the centre of the chest begins. (W6 & 7)*

8. *The hands cross the centre of the chest. The body begins to turn. The rear foot moves back and begins to take weight. (W9)*

<u>*Always*</u>, *when punting standing still, the forward foot should be against the side of the punt, preferably against a knee, and <u>should never move from that position</u>.*
*In position 1, the finish, there is an error in the drawing, the pole resting on the punter's shoulder; the pole should touch the outside of the shoulder.*

## Double Punting

Double punting was at one time a common practice in pleasure punting. It is of course still a usual event in punt racing. Pleasure punts would often carry a spare pole slung in leather straps over the side of the punt; this could be used for double punting. For a long trip, double punting can considerably reduce the physical effort needed for it. The rhythm developed from good timing can give the punters a great deal of pleasure and satisfaction.

For double punting, the punters may punt from opposite sides or from the same side. Punting from the same side is better; punting from opposite sides is less efficient, since the punt lies flat on the water and does not have the keel to give directional stability obtained by keeping the weight on one side; nor does it so well assist good timing. Bow gives the timing of the stroke and the stern man is mainly responsible for steering; otherwise for steering, bow pole shoves around and the stern pole pinches the punt.

A beginner may do well in learning to punt by double punting with a skilful and considerate punter. A beginner double punting should punt at bow; the stern man should be competent to keep in time whatever timing is given and should undertake the steering. (When the beginner starts learning to steer from stern position, it may help at first for bow to put in two strokes to stern's one, and correct the direction on the alternate stroke.) In double punt racing, perfect timing is required, particularly in moving the foot. To stop up, bow gives a signal to stop punting and turn. Stern then becomes bow, and must give a signal or call for throwing down the poles: the poles must strike the bottom simultaneously and at the same angle.

## Punting Facing Forward

This technique is sometimes to be seen and is common at Cambridge when the punter stands on the stern. It is mechanically less efficient than standing square to the side; it would only be used by a professional Thames waterman when manoeuvering a punt in a limited space. There were no professional watermen who taught punting when it was introduced at Cambridge and undergraduates developed *ad hoc* a method most convenient for novices. A leading professional Cambridge waterman was in fact taught the Thames style of punting by an undergraduate from Maidenhead when punts were introduced there, and the Thames style appears to have been used almost only by undergraduates who had first learnt to punt on the Thames. When standing square to the front, the pole can be brought up in three, but the shove consists of a pull without the push or after-shove that follows in the full stroke; the stroke is mechanically lengthened a little sometimes by bending the knees and pulling the hands down to the feet, the recovery being made with a spring upwards which may rock the punt. The technique is not effective for racing because the stroke is too short, lacking a back-shove; nor does the pole travel for long enough along the side for steering-leverage. Steering must therefore be done by trailing the pole over the stern, losing both time and momentum from pole-drag.

## One-Armed Punting

This was once a popular technique used in less serious regattas. The punter stands facing squarely forward and brings up the pole by throwing it forward two or three times to the point of balance where it can be tilted with a wrist movement. Reaching the vertical, the pole balances easily and can drop. Steering during the shove is not difficult.

At the end of the shove, direction can also be corrected with a small twist of the wrist when the pole has floated to the surface. Keep the feet still throughout, but bend the knees to create a rhythm.

## Punting with Hands Low

This is a technique which was used for pleasure punting in the 1890's, and possibly developed earlier; for Leslie mentioned the importance of keeping the hands low in order to keep the wrists dry, in *Our River*. The technique contrasts with that of the conventional stroke for punting at pressure, for it has a simple, single purpose which decides the matter of style: to produce the maximum mechanical efficiency with the minimum of physical effort, effortlessness receiving first attention. In the days when men punted with starched cuffs, the technique was valuable for keeping the wrists dry. From a distance, a punter using the technique might appear almost motionless and certainly effortless. The technique is excellent practice for maintaining an upright posture.

The technique may be learnt by following this strict drill: both arms are stretched at full length downwards and the hands are bent up at right angles to the wrists. For practice, the whole stroke can be made with the hands well below the waist; the effort is worth attempting. A well shaped and balanced pole, tapered towards the top, helps. Hold the pole precisely horizontal and test its balance. Hold it with the rear hand over it; and with the forward hand over when the point of balance is to the rear of the rear hand, and under it when it is forward of the rear hand. Keep the point of balance near the rear hand. With the point of balance carefully controlled, the pole will swing easily to the vertical position with a downward pressure of the rear hand and an upward pressure of the forward, the arms still stretched well downwards. After the pole is dropped, the shove can be made with the arms low and the wrists bent up; when the pole has floated to the surface, the recovery is made hand to hand in their lowest position.

The stroke may be made at greater pressure after the drop, still keeping the wrists dry, by pulling on the pole with the rear hand first, and then as the body passes the pole, the forward hand following it at waist height; the rear hand following again, until the pole has passed to its full length. This is in fact "climbing the pole", though on a horizontal plane. The forward hand can grip the end of the pole as it floats to the surface with the wrist over the end of it, a grip similar to the forward hand on a cricket bat. With the hands low, the recovery may be made vigorously, accelerating on the second movement. Then if as the pole is accelerated, the forward hand, held open, is brought sharply back and slightly downwards as the pole accelerates, it lifts quickly and effortlessly to the position for the drop, with the forearms at waist height. When the technique is completely mastered, it is no more effort to punt sitting down than standing up. If the punter has gone on the river to be idle, this allows longer periods between strokes than would be needed with a paddle. The pole can be held with the hand resting on the side between strokes, its weight carried by the water. The recovery can be made with the forward hand resting on the side, the pole sliding over the fingers as they droop below the side. A brief acceleration will lift the pole as the slightly open forward hand is pulled back against it. Steering during the stroke is easy because of the forward position of the punter in the punt. The punter is out of any difficulties made by a cross-wind, and the occasional shove with a pole requires considerably less effort than the constant use of a paddle.

## Rotating the Pole

The "windmill" stroke made by rotating the pole, with alternate ends striking the bottom, is occasionally seen. It should not be encouraged without a special pole for it, since this could damage the unshod end. In water about a foot deep, the windmill stroke would be in theory very efficient made with a special suitable short pole, but there is very little water suitable for it. The stroke has been tried on part of the present Chertsey course just above the old Shepperton course. American canoe-polers have experimented with the windmill stroke. A three-quarter rotation of the pole can be used for stopping-up, the shoe passing overhead. A former Thames Punting Champion used to make several windmill strokes at the end of a less serious race to indicate he had won. Abel Beesley is said once to have rotated the pole when he had a very unequal competitor and also stopped to talk to the spectators.

## Grappling Punts

Several punts together can be moved by one punter if they are grappled by the passengers or tied together by painters. If grappled, the best place to hold is near the forward back-rests. A number of punts held together thus can be double punted from opposite sides. To travel a long distance it is easier to tie the punts together with their painters. This is called rafting them.

## Punting a Dinghy

In the right circumstances, a waterman may handle most craft with a pole and should feel he will do so without difficulty. A dinghy is the craft he is most likely to handle thus. How it is handled will depend on its design; but many dinghies are more easily punted stern first. At one time in children's regattas, punting dinghies stern first was a popular event, and many young watermen learnt to punt this way.

In water suitable for it, a dinghy is more manoeuverable when handled with a pole than with oars or sculls. The waterman looks ahead and can also see easily all around him; the pole occupies only a few inches of space around the craft, whereas oars or sculls extend to double their length around it; with a pole, the waterman can make small and precise movements; though not suitable for speed or distance, paddling with the pole can replace shoving in an unexpected depth or mud patch. A seaman calls a pole used for this purpose a "sprit"; the word "spar" is more often used for timber in standing or permanent rigging.

## Hints on Punting

H.M. Winstanley ended his book *Punting* with a few hints. They include: "Learn swimming before punting... Never go out in a punt without a spare pole or paddle. If your pole sticks hard in mud, let go! You can go back and fetch it... If you come to deep water, and have no paddle, you can paddle quite well with the pole... When you want to turn your punt round, let the stream help you. When you are going upstream, put the bow out into the stream and it will swing round of its own accord. Similarly, if you are going downstream, put the stern out into the stream... If you don't want to get wet, in lifting your pole out and dropping it into the water, use your fingers, not your whole hands."

Other writers on punting emphasize the importance of punting with the fingers. As far as possible, effort should be concentrated in them more than in the limbs and trunk. It is a good practice occasionally to punt with the fingers only in order to check the faults in style it can eliminate. With regard to keeping dry, A.E. Banham wrote, "if, in recovering and holding the pole, the backs of the wrists are kept up and the fingers and thumbs droop downwards, the punter should keep entirely free from the spray-bath effects when going at a moderate pace." He did not mean facing upwards, but high; the grip may be overhand or underhand, but the wrist position must be found to make the hands droop, as a pianist's hands should droop from the wrists. Handling the pole with the fingers only is another exercise suitable for practise on dry land, with the arms relaxed and the body upright.

A cross wind can affect steering and cause a good deal of difficulty, even for an experienced punter. The wind catches the area of surface of the body at the stern like a sail, turning it towards the lee bank, and the head of the punt into the wind. In a strong wind, the whole of the punt may move towards the lee bank as well. A beginner should therefore avoid learning in a cross wind. In difficulty, it may be well to use paddles.

## Safety in Punting

Accidents in punting occur, and in recent years there have been deaths by drowning from punts. With good watermanship, moderate competence and a knowledge of conditions of danger and how to deal with them, punting is perfectly safe. Cambridge has a better safety record than Oxford; the fact that the river most used for punting at Cambridge passes through college gardens and the town and is better watched may help, but it is still liable to fast streams in flood water.

Deaths by drowning have been caused by drunkenness; those going on the river to drink must bear in mind that they may hazard a life; in one case, it was found that members of such a party could not afterwards tell the coroner how or when one of them who had drowned was missed; in such circumstances, therefore, danger is possible when little expected.

There are two conditions of danger from the stream. The first is a swollen stream, one found in spring or after prolonged heavy rainfall. If the punt gets out of control because of a fast flowing stream, it can be quickly, strongly and unexpectedly swung, and the punter who does not bring the pole to a position of safety is in danger. However, punt-hirers now usually prohibit the use of punts in a dangerous stream. The second danger is that for a punter surprised by falling in; if the water, again often in a swollen stream is murky he may lose his sense of direction, even if only briefly; danger is greater if he is carried under branches or vegetation.

Everyone punting should be able to swim; but surprise can add to danger and a punter should, from time to time, imagine what he would do if he or a passenger fell in. Anyone who falls in does so almost certainly because of a momentary over-exertion of some part of the body. The over-exertion preceding the fall can confuse and disconcert adding even more to the danger. If you have reason to believe you may fall, relax and make plans. It is better to fall in deliberately under control than later out of control. Fall feet first, take your bearings and decide in advance where you are going to swim to. The fact you do this may relax you enough to put you in a position of safety again. Experience of swimming fully dressed in a river is worth having. Some boat clubs have required members to swim in a mackintosh and boots. Another rule taught is, always to swim to the boat.

There are two conditions of danger concerned with the punter's style: first, punting with a foot away from the side, and secondly gripping the pole too hard. These are both natural faults for a beginner. They can become habitual and be incorporated into a style; for a style of punting once acquired and adhered to because it works, may be difficult to change.

With regard to the first danger, the novice should concentrate on keeping the centre of gravity of the pole outside or at least above the edge of the punt, not inside it. The further inside the punt it comes, the more dangerous it will be in a moment of danger. A novice sometimes tries to balance the punt so it is level crossways, believing it will help his balance; but it will not. A good exercise for establishing balance (one recommended to beginners by Winstanley), is to keep the toes of both feet against the side of the punt and to rock it gently until the feel of balance comes, from the toes, the ankles and legs, always being relaxed and "giving" at the knees. The knees and ankles should absorb all the movements of the punt like "shock absorbers" so that the upper body remains balanced and steady.

The second danger is probably the greatest of all, and the most serious – gripping the pole unnecessarily hard. This arises from the increase of body tension. It may be recognized or unrecognized. It may eventually cause so strong a grip on the pole that the punter can hardly move his arms, and so compulsive that the punter releases his hands with difficulty. It is very important to learn to relax the hands and fingers or reduce their tension at the end of every stroke as part of your style and technique. Tension, particularly in the hands, also causes the crouching, stooping or bending of the body or knees that is dangerous. It is often more apparent to an onlooker than to the punter. Anticipating danger in a punt, straighten your body and relax your arms immediately. This brings you at once to the position of greatest safety. Then bring the pole from wherever you are holding it to the lowest point at which you can hold it. Indeed, the reflex on touching a pole at any time when not making a stroke, should be to bring or slide the fingers to reach the lowest point at which it can be held. Let the pole float on the water, astern. In this position you can hold it with a finger tip only, if you wish; hold it with the least effort possible. Straighten your body. A safe position now is the "mid-recovery" position with the hands apart in front of the body and the pole at about 45°. When you are motionless and upright, begin to think what action is necessary. It may be a half shove. It may be to swing the punt with the pole. More important, however, is to maintain your posture and to eliminate unnecessary effort in action. Using more effort than you require is one of the principal causes of danger in punting and causes tension to increase. In a position of danger you will be safe with your hands at their lowest position.

There are two minor causes of danger in punting that should not provide difficulty: mud and tree-branches. If you have difficulty with mud, it is because you are using too much effort. Punt lightly with your fingers; develop a feel for the river bottom that comes through the use of the fingers. If there is no slight vibration as the pole strikes the bottom, beware that it may be soft. The best technique for punting in mud is to lean forward and put the pole into the water at 45° backwards. Push only gently. The combination of angle and a quick twist and tug will release the pole. If it goes in vertically, it will sink deeper into mud: therefore (I) low angle, (2) half-shove only, (3) light pressure, (4) twist and tug.

If the mud is hindering your progress, do not hesitate to use your pole like a canoe-paddle till you have passed it.

Looking well ahead, you can keep clear of most tree branches. If you have to punt under them, be sure to keep momentum in the movement of the punt and choose the right moment to give a shove towards them; then, holding the pole down at the second movement of the pick up, at the mid-recovery position, wait for a suitable place in the branches to lift the pole between them. When racing punts are crowded together, poles for safety should be brought to the vertical. This is a safe position also for the heavy pleasure punt pole, especially on land. Learn to hold the pole near its bottom, balanced vertically without support from the shoulder, hanging from your fingers with your arms stretched down.

## The Rule of the Road

At sea or on inland waterways in every part of the world, the rule of the road is to keep to the right of oncoming craft. Most other rules are based on common sense; for example, a boat overtaking keeps clear of the boat it is overtaking, holds its course and speed and avoids crossing ahead.

At Oxford and Cambridge, by punting left-handed, that is to say, on the right as one faces forward, it is easier to follow the narrow streams of the Cherwell and Cam facing the bank, and the bank to the right is the correct one to follow. This may explain why it is customary on the Cherwell and Cam to punt left-handed. At one time the Thames Conservancy byelaws provided rules for punts. Their most recent navigation byelaws, those of 1957, omit them. In 1895 the rules said: "*Boats going against the stream.* – A rowing boat or punt going against the stream or tide has the right to either shore or bank, and should keep inside all craft meeting it (except barges towing). When going against stream or tide, and overtaking another craft, a rowing boat or punt should keep outside the craft overtaken." For boats going with the stream, the rule is the converse; but there is the following addition: "it would undoubtedly be a concession of considerable advantage to a punt to be allowed to pass on the inside close to the shore, more particularly in places where the river is deep in the middle ... when going down stream punts should never claim to go on the inside as a right, but only take that position if the skiff is inclined to make way for them."

On rivers that are rowed on, punts can present difficulties to eight-oared, four-oared and uncoxed boats. Oarsmen prefer punts to keep to the banks, though boats will themselves sometimes come in to a bank. A good cox, in the interests of good watermanship, is keenly aware of all around him. If you have any doubt of a boat not seeing you or giving you room, shout early and very loudly, "Look out ahead!"

Give consideration to other punts, especially beginners who are trying to avoid you. If you are not certain of the course of an oncoming punt, hold your course to see how it will pass. Steer to pass it on the opposite side to your pole. The control of the situation will remain with the punt making the last shove; therefore delay your shove if in doubt. Give an oncoming punt as much room as it needs and always steer to avoid a collision if possible. If the other punt touches you, and you have delayed your shove, you will then have momentum to stay on course and very gently but precisely push the other punt aside, by steering against its weight, shoving around or pinching your punt to the degree to stay exactly on your course; do not push it further than you need for this. If you are compelled to make a shove within touching distance of another punt, it may be better to make a half-shove, not a full-shove, to keep the reserve of power it can give.

# The History of Punts

## *Pleasure Punts Today*

The pleasure punts of today were unknown before 1860. They reached their greatest popularity in Edward VII's reign (1901–1910). Between 1950 and 1970, they were driven off most rivers by the wash of increasing numbers of motor boats which rocked or swamped them. Today they are found almost only at Oxford and Cambridge on rivers protected for them. In 1939 there were 1,600 licensed motor boats on the Thames: in 1978, 13,000, an increase of eightfold. On other rivers the increase has also been substantial. The only pleasure punts remaining for hire without previous arrangements, except at Oxford and Cambridge, are six at Stratford-on-Avon (Rose), four, one a mahogany fishing punt, at Henley-on-Thames (Hooper), two Thames and four Medway 46 in-wide punts at Godalming, Surrey on the Wey, and a few small punts at Houghton Mill near St Ives on the Great Ouse. There are still a number of privately owned punts. At Durham University, four colleges each have a punt on one of the most beautiful stretches of river in England

## The Thames Punt

The punt is a traditional Thames craft. Its design may be unique. There are many small, square-ended craft throughout the world, but their frames are usually box-shaped. The frame of the Thames punt, however, is like a ladder. Broad cross-pieces called "treads" join the two sides together across its bottom; this is structurally its frame. The treads at Oxford only are called "rounds", the name for the cross-braces between chair legs. A punt's bottom is made of soft wood and may be replaced several times during its lifetime. The sides of a pleasure punt are made of mahogany and the treads of teak. The treads and sides are joined by braces called "knees". A pleasure punt usually has eleven treads, is 24 ft – 26 ft long and 32 in – 34 in wide. A few punts were built with 13 treads and were 26 ft – 28 ft long. The ends are called "huffs". The bottom, with planks lengthways, is built first, shaped with slopes at each end called "swims", the treads and knees are fixed to it and then the sides. The knees are either upright or "raked" or

SHOES FOR PUNT POLES
Plug Shoe for Racing (obsolete)
Mud Shoe

RAKED KNEES

Old Fashioned Shoe
Modern Shoe

STERN    SALOON with Cushions    BOW

Huff    Till or Box (Oxford) or Deck (Cambridge)    Knee (upright)    After Back Rest    Grating    Forward Back Rest    Tread    Huff

Swim    Swim    Painter

A THAMES PLEASURE PUNT

sloped; the sole purpose of raked knees is to improve the appearance. Between the treads, the floor is covered with "gratings". If a punt was narrow (as all pleasure punts are), the stern was covered with wood to strengthen the frame. This covering is called the "till" or sometimes (at Oxford only) the "box" and (at Cambridge) the "deck".

A racing punt, being even narrower, is covered at both ends; its coverings are called "counters".

The Thames Punting Club provides this useful definition of a punt in the rules of punt racing: "A punt is a flat-bottomed craft without stem, keel or sternpost, and the width at each end must be at least one-half of the width at the widest point. The length of a punt is its extreme measurement over all, and its width is its extreme part measured inside on the bottom. Subject to compliance with these definitions, a punt may be any length or width." The correct waterman's term for punting is "shoving", still used in punt racing.

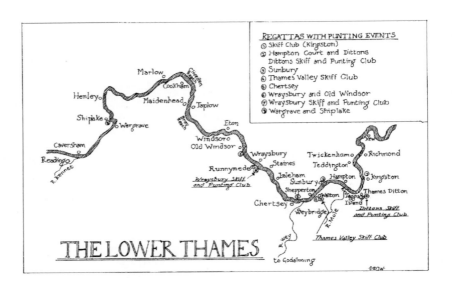

## Different Kinds of Punts

Until 1770, the Thames was much shallower than now. A great deal of its bottom is gravel. The punt was a useful craft then, easy to manoeuvre, capacious and able to move in very shallow water. After 1770, river improvements began. More and better locks were built to control its depth, and channels were dredged for navigation and to contain the water in floods. Punts of different kinds were used for different tasks. The largest were barges, sometimes with a sail, able to sail in the shallow parts of the Thames estuary and over the mud flats of the east coast, and called at sea "swimmies". Before the building of bridges, there were many ferry punts of different sizes. Ballast punts dredged gravel, valuable for road making and building, from the river bed. Watermen used punts for transporting goods between houses and villages along the river when it was more suitable for this than roads. Work punts were used for the repair of river banks and locks. Finally, there were many fishermen working on the river until fish stocks diminished. Net fishing was prohibited by the Thames Conservancy, founded in 1857. Fishermen used a special design of punt, the fishing punt.

The word "punt" was originally used for any small craft. A number of its uses were replaced during the 19th century by the word "dinghy", introduced from Bengal. By the early 20th century its use was largely restricted to the Thames craft. Some examples of its older use are "gun punt", an obsolete, canoe-shaped, clinker-built wildfowler's craft (surviving as a Norfolk club sailing boat) and "Falmouth quay punt", a Cornish design of fishing yawl. A "duck punt" is a small, stemmed, flat-bottomed, sculling boat.

## Punt Poles

Poles are used to shove craft of various kinds on inland waters in many parts of the world. They are especially useful for handling heavy canoes on rapid rivers. The broadland "quant" and Dutch *stok* differ from punt poles in having cross pieces at the top to place under the armpit when shoving. The first punt poles were heavy larch spars, roughly cut. The first pleasure punt poles were spruce, shaped and varnished, like today's. Racing poles weighed about 4½ lbs and were West Virginia spruce, a wood not available since 1936. From 1946, aluminium poles weighing 3¼ – 3½ lbs have been used for racing. The Lower Thames being shallow, poles used there were 13 – 14ft. A rough guide to depth was that above Cookham the Thames was deeper, and below it shallower, dredged channels excepted. Both at Oxford and Cambridge poles are 16 ft and weigh 9–10½ lbs; they are all made by F. Collar of South Hinksey, Oxford. At Oxford some aluminium poles are used of the same weight and length. A leaky aluminium pole, being hollow, fills with water and becomes heavier. The end of the pole is fitted with a metal "shoe". The earliest shoes were forked. The usual shoe now is of a double horned shape, supposed to prevent the picking up of stones. A fluted half-disc shoe is called a mud shoe, though on mud how the pole is used is more important than the shape of the shoe. For use on hard gravel, some racing poles had a rounded end called a plug shoe.

## Fishing Punts

Today's pleasure punts and racing punts both originate from the fishing punt. The fishing punt was 24–25 ft long and 42–46 in wide. It had a short till and forward of the till, about one-third of the way along the punt, was a "wet well". The wet well was a watertight box across the width of the punt, about a foot wide, the same height as the punt and covered with a lid. At either end of the box, holes in the side of the punt flooded it with water; in it was kept the fisherman's live bait and sometimes catches of fish or eels. The fishing punt was built of oak, often tarred on the bottom, and was traditionally painted green. It was not built for movement, was wide enough to hold three chairs and was moored all day for fishing to poles called "rye pecks". There are now only four traditional, oak fishing punts left on the Thames, at Sunbury. The last statutory ferry punt shoved with a pole is also at Sunbury, but it is rarely used now.

## The First Pleasure Punts

In the second part of the 19th century the railways made the Thames valley much more accessible to residents of the rapidly growing city of London. It became a popular place for recreation and residence by those who could travel to and from London. Residents beside the river began to have fishing punts built of mahogany, varnished not painted, for their own recreation. These varnished, mahogany fishing punts were lighter than oak punts and served the dual purpose of fishing and travelling for pleasure; the second purpose was often the more popular because, being light, they were easy to move. If passengers were carried, a mattress was placed against the till and sometimes also against the wet well (kept dry in a pleasure punt when not fishing). It was not until the 1880's that the "saloon" punt was invented with the seating design used today for four passengers or "sitters" looking inwards, leaning against "back-rests" and with specially fitted cushions to sit on.

## Walking and Pricking a Punt

The building of lighter punts meant that it was possible to punt them standing still. This is called "pricking" the punt. The heavy oak punt was "walked" or "run". The punter dropped in the pole at the bow of the punt and walked down it at least three paces, pushing or "shoving" with the pole. This was very often necessary for handling a heavy punt. When the first pleasure punts were pricked, it was usual to punt stern first, from the open end opposite the till. In 1898, P.W. Squire, secretary of the Thames Punting Club, comparing the old type of punt with the new saloon punt, wrote "When the lounge cushion is placed against the 'till' or covered-in end of the punt, as in the old-fashioned style, the craft is usually propelled stern first." At Oxford, men continued to punt stern first after the saloon design of punt was introduced, and it is now traditional at Oxford to do so. Lord Desborough noted that when Abel Beesley first won the professional championship in 1878 by pricking his punt, he punted stern first. There are certain advantages in it for a learner also.    The saloon punt was probably more popular at first on the Lower Thames. Pleasure punts were not introduced to Cambridge till after 1900 and always have been of the saloon design only; like Thames punts outside Oxford, they were punted bow first, but not always from behind the after back-rest. Punters at Cambridge often stood on the till or deck, a position of advantage for beginners. Punting stern first is sometimes called punting from the "Oxford end" and bow first, from the "Cambridge end".

## Early Punt Racing and the Giants of the Sport

Both professional watermen and amateurs raced punts from early in the 19th century. Punt racing was very popular at Eton College until 1852 when it was prohibited because punts were believed to be used for school vices, smoking and drinking. The first professional championship of the Thames was held over a one-mile course at Maidenhead in 1877, the Maidenhead Mile. The same course was used for it until the championship finished in 1953. The greatest professional punter of all time was Abel Beesley, an Oxford Waterman. The greatest of amateur punters was W.H. Grenfell, later 1st Lord Desborough, the "Grand Old Man of almost every kind of sport". He was president of the Oxford University Athletic and Boat Clubs, broke his school's half-mile record, twice swam the pool below Niagara Falls, made the ascent of five Alpine peaks in eight days, captained the British épée fencing team at the age of 49 and was president of the M.C.C., the L.T.A. and of the 1908 Olympic Games. He and Abel Beesley, his coach, are given the credit of establishing punt racing as a recognized sport.

The greatest of women punters was Penny Chuter, ladies' amateur punting champion from 1957 to 1966, daughter of a retired naval officer at Laleham-on-Thames. She began skiff racing in 1958, best boat racing in 1959 and in 1960, aged 17, was placed 4th in the European Ladies' Sculling Championship as a member of the Laleham Skiff and Punting Club (since closed). She is now Senior National (A.R.A.) Men's Rowing Coach.

## The Thames Punting Club

The Thames Punting Club was founded in 1887 at Sunbury-on-Thames. It took responsibility for the government of the sport of punt racing and organized an amateur punting championship. Grenfell reorganized the club in 1890 and in 1895 the club found an excellent punting course near Shepperton for its annual championship regattas. The course was inadvertently dredged in 1936 and lost; the regattas were held subsequently at Staines, Maidenhead and Laleham and were concluded in 1969 when competitors of sufficient standard were lacking. However, punt racing has continued by members of skiff and punting clubs affiliated to the Thames Punting Club in regattas held in August and September after the main rowing season has finished.

## The Skiff and Punting Clubs

There are four clubs affiliated to the Thames Punting Club (the Thames Punting Club is also affiliated to the Amateur Rowing Association and the Skiff Racing Association). Punt racing is a very local sport, limited to the Thames from Wargrave below Reading to Teddington at the head of the London tideway, a distance of about thirty miles. There are about eight or nine annual regattas with punting events. The Dittons S.P.C. At Thames Ditton opposite Hampton Court; the Thames

Valley S.C. at Walton-on-Thames, and the Wraysbury S.P.C. at the east end of Runnymede are skiff and punting clubs. The Wargrave Boat Club is a social club with punt racing included in its activities. Anyone interested in seriously training for punt racing would be welcomed in a skiff and punting club, especially if competent in a pleasure punt and even more if experienced in punting a canoe. Annual subscriptions with use of boats are from £10 to £20. The clubs are open on Sundays, with two club evenings a week in the winter and four in the summer. There is an annual Inter-Club Punting Championship. It is hoped the amateur championship may be restarted.

## Punt Racing

There are two types of racing punts: 2 ft wide punts for novice and doubles racing, and "best and best" punts for seniors and championships. The word best-and-best is an old boatbuilder's term for the best obtainable of the kind of boat required, not matched, as the 2ft punts are. A best and best punt is about 14 ½ in wide and 32–35 ft long. A punt racing course is 660–880 yards with a turn, so only half this distance of the river is used. The course should be shallow and firm, about 3–4 ft deep. The events are held in heats and the punts race in pairs. They are started from a stake-punt and turn at two poles called ryepecks, shod with iron points, planted in the river. Racing punts are double-ended, with both ends identical and are shoved from the centre. On passing the ryepeck, the punter "stops up", or stops the punt with his pole, reverses his direction (the bow becomes the stern) and passes up-stream on the other side of the ryepeck to finish where the race began at the ryepecks that were holding the stake-punt.

## Dongola Racing

Exciting and popular events in punts are dongola races: the punts are paddled. The name commemorates Lord Wolseley's unsuccessful Nile Expedition of 1884–5 to relieve General Gordon at Khartum. Wolseley had 800 naval Whalers built, crewed by soldiers, with teams of Canadian voyageurs to help them at the many rapids and cataracts on the hazardous journey up to the head of the province of Dongola. He offered a prize of £100 to the first battalion to complete the 370 mile journey. *The Times* described it as "The longest boat race in history". The first dongola race was held at Maidenhead in 1886, with crews of eight, four aside with canoe paddles. A dongola crew today is usually six, mixed, four men and two women. The major trophy is the African World Shield, competed for at the Sunbury Regatta. At the Wargrave and Shiplake Regatta in 1981 there were entries from no less than 62 dongola crews. Dongola racing is traditionally light-hearted and crews often sink a punt at the end of the races, but serious dongola racing can produce displays of fine watermanship.

## Long Distance Punting

In recent years, undergraduates from both Oxford and Cambridge have set up long distance punting records travelling mainly on canals, using camping punts, popular 70 years ago. Their reports are favourable and it may be that outside Oxford and Cambridge the most hopeful future for pleasure punts will be on canals. Most canals have a firm bottom for much of their width and at the few places where a bank is muddy there is always a hard bottom in the centre of the canal. There is an even depth at a convenient 6–8 feet. The reaches are straight. River traffic is slow, creating no problems with wash. As compared with some owners and hirers of river launches, the users of the canals are considerate, polite and usually show interest in traditional craft.

A camping punt is an ordinary pleasure punt with removable hoops 4 ft high; fitted canvas is unrolled over the hoops to turn the punt into a tent at night; the cushions fit the floor between the back-rests to make a mattress.

Printed in Great Britain
by Amazon

38127558R00070